W9-BFZ-075

Searching
for
Sacred
Space

Searching for Sacred Space

ESSAYS ON ARCHITECTURE AND LITURGICAL DESIGN IN THE EPISCOPAL CHURCH

John Ander Runkle
Editor

 CHURCH

Church Publishing Incorporated, New York

Copyright © 2002 by the editor and contributors
All rights reserved.

"A,a,a, Domine Deus" from *The Sleeping Lord* by David Jones.
Used by permission of Faber & Faber LTD.

"Church Going" from *Philip Larkin: Collected Poems.*
Used by permission of George Hartley.

Library of Congress Cataloging-in-Publication Data

Searching for sacred space : essays on architecture and liturgical design
in the Episcopal Church / John Ander Runkle, editor.
    p. cm.
  Includes bibliographical references.
  ISBN:0-89869-371-3 (pbk.)
    1. Anglican church buildings. 2. Liturgy and architecture.
3. Episcopal Church. I. Runkle, John Ander.

NA4829.A6 S43 2002
246'.9583--dc21

2002031546

Church Publishing Incorporated
445 Fifth Avenue
New York, NY 10016
www.churchpublishing.org

5 4 3 2 1

Contents

SEARCHING FOR SACRED SPACE

Acknowledgments

A publication of this nature is possible only through the contributions of a great many people. The Rt. Rev. Dr. Neil Alexander, the Rev. Dr. Marion Hatchett, and the Very Rev. Dr. Guy Lytle, as my professors in seminary, refused to let me forget that architecture was my first calling and the important role it offers to the life of the church. The Rev. Tom Ward, as spiritual guide, companion and friend, shares the walk along the path of ordination and life. Dr. James Dunkly models integrity in his passion for the art and craft of the written word. Mr. Frank Tedeschi, Managing Editor, indulged my desire to fashion such a book and made the endeavor possible. Each of the contributing writers who, for their love of the church and despite their many other pressing demands, found time to express their thoughts and feelings so eloquently, in spite of my relentless badgering. The Rev. Deborah Hentz Hunley and the people of Christ Episcopal Church in Roanoke, Virginia, graciously allowed and encouraged me to pursue this project. Ms. Denita Wray, Office Manager at Christ Episcopal Church, cheerfully typed my requests, answered phone calls, and solved all my computer problems throughout this undertaking. To each of you, I am extremely grateful.

Finally, my deepest appreciation and affection goes to Harriet, my personal editor, most honest and severe critic, ardent supporter, closest friend, and dearest companion for life who, as I shared with her hearing the call to ordained life, cried, "I didn't marry a priest; I married an architect!" Without her love, neither are possible.

John Ander Runkle
Roanoke, Virginia
The Feast of Catherine of Siena, 2002

Introduction

John Ander Runkle

In his celebrated poem, *Four Quartets,* T.S. Eliot strives to capture the essence of places he has found sacred, places where he has experienced the Incarnation of God. Of the four, perhaps one of the most memorable images comes from *Little Gidding.* Located in the English countryside, Little Gidding is both a place and a religious community with roots in the seventeenth century. For Eliot, the meaning of Little Gidding came from the church building itself and the use to which it had been put. In the poem, he seeks to draw the reader into his experience with such statements as, "You are here to kneel where prayer has been valid." His image calls to mind a general truth, an experience many have shared, yet have not often formed into words. His words conjure in us memories of places where we have experienced God, places that have invited and compelled us into robust conversations with God. This is not to say these places made our prayers efficacious, but they inspired us, shaped our beliefs, assured us in our relationship with God, and helped that relationship grow.

Such places do not come into being by accident. They are created by our intentional actions that focus and concentrate our devotion to God in specific locations. These actions spring forth from our individual and collective hopes and desires, and are made visible through architectural forms and spaces crafted with sincerity, creativity, and cooperation.

As a priest, I do not doubt the Episcopal Church's desire to have such "valid" places of worship. But as an architect, I grow increasingly concerned about our ability to create them. The following essays are written by individuals who share this concern, people from within the Episcopal Church and other Christian traditions who see the potential for our church buildings to be places to experience the Incarnation of

God.

The general state of architecture and liturgical design in the Episcopal Church is in decline. Once known for its architectural leadership, our tradition now has many existing church buildings growing ever more dysfunctional to the needs of the people and its liturgy. Most new designs are superficial, either mimicking styles of days gone by or serving as self-absorbed, personal statements of a designer's ego. The Episcopal Church appears content to wander in an architectural wilderness. The desire to move beyond this apathetic state and create church buildings relevant to our time rarely is seen. We seem to have forgotten the importance—the role and meaning—church buildings have in our tradition. We are avoiding answering such questions as:

- How do our buildings convey a vision of God's kingdom on earth?
- How are our places of worship reflecting our beliefs?
- In what visible, tangible forms are we proclaiming a faith in the living God?
- How are our church buildings helping this church bring the gospel into a new century?

Today, the Episcopal Church is called to serve in a culture that is highly attuned to visual media. Unfortunately, our most prevalent and visible public symbol, the church building, often appears as quaint, irrelevant, or worse—completely invisible.

One can cite a variety of reasons for this problem, ranging from theological to financial, but the primarily problem is neglect. Throughout much of the twentieth century, the Episcopal Church did not educate itself on the meaning and importance of thoughtful, evocative church architecture. We abdicated our responsibility to create high-quality buildings, deferring instead to the design professionals, very few of whom are adequately grounded in our liturgy, our theology, our ecclesiology, and our tradition. As a result, our years of complacency now are bearing bitter fruit.

Of course, if you ask anyone in the church what makes for good design, most will give an opinion. Yet, rarely are such opinions of informed substance. Most are shaped by romantic notions or limited personal experience, rather than collective reasoned reflection. In order for our places of worship to convey any sense of relevance, they must be created from a deliberate, honest self-understanding of who we are and what we believe. As David Stancliffe argues in his essay in this collection, "there must be a known relationship between the symbolic significance of the building and the use to which that space is put." Such expressions can only take place through communities that are involved and informed.

Part of the problem stems from the limited resources available within the Episcopal Church for learning about church building design. Few opportunities exist for courses to be taught, questions answered, opinions shared, issues debated, or alternative approaches considered. Individuals and building committees are forced to look to other Christian traditions for guidance—from books, periodicals, conferences, videos, and websites. To be sure, isolated pockets of conversation take place within the church—at the parish level, in the seminaries, and among concerned design professionals—but rarely do such thoughts and feelings extend beyond each respective community. Little ongoing work is being done on a concerted, church-wide level to draw such voices together, to provide opportunities for learning from and sharing experiences with others. Whether at the diocesan, parochial, or individual level, we are left to make design decisions with limited understanding or advice.

As David Smart points out in his essay, there exists, within the Episcopal Church and our broader Anglican heritage, a history that whenever the state of architecture falls in need, the church responds to the occasion. Regardless of whether or not one prefers the architectural expression of a particular age, it is evident that leadership was shown. As the English church adjusted to the sixteenth-century Reformation, the former Roman Catholic places of worship had to be reordered to accommodate the new liturgy that allowed the laity to participate more fully. In the seventeenth century, after much of the city of London burned, the English church used the talents of Christopher Wren and Nicholas Hawksmoor to help design new worship spaces more attuned to the increasing auditory needs of the gathered assembly.[1] In the nineteenth century, as a response to a perceived decline in ecclesial piety and enthusiasm, the Cambridge Ecclesiologists initiated a vigorous program of liturgical and architectural education whose influence was felt, not only in the Church of England and the Episcopal Church, but also throughout most of Western Christianity.[2] Finally, during the mid-twentieth century, as the wave of the liturgical movement swept through Western churches, passionate voices within the Episcopal Church and the Church of England called for the church to recognize the relevance of this movement and allow its church buildings to reflect it.

Peter Hammond was one such voice. He roused Anglican attention on both sides of the Atlantic with his arguments for the need of relevant church buildings.[3] In his book *Towards a Church Architecture* (1962), Hammond draws together a variety of voices contending that the church needs to create coherent designs and engage the potential that modern architecture has on its buildings. Making no attempt to reconcile opposing views between the contributors or to present a unified opinion, Hammond instead sought to heighten awareness within the church, to stimulate discussion, and to raise fundamental questions that would result in more intentional, honest, and useful places of worship. Many heard the call, agreeing with it in principle, but few attempts were made to put it into practice. That was forty years ago, and the Episcopal Church has made little effort since then to perpetuate or advance the discussion.

With this book, it is my hope, and that of the contributors, to resume the discussion where Hammond left off, to rekindle concern within the church about the importance of our buildings, and to assist in educating our members. Using Hammond's book as a model, this collection brings many voices together, voices from across the Episcopal Church, the Anglican Communion, and other Christian traditions. Each writer brings a passion for our places of worship and sees this work as an opportunity for a cross-pollination to take place that will help resuscitate, invigorate, and strengthen the future yield of inspiring church buildings.

As with Hammond's book, no attempt is made to resolve opposing views here. No one particular form, style, or theory of architecture is promoted above another. No absolutes are contained or implied within. The Episcopal Church is much too pluralistic for that.[4] It is the work of each congregation to wrestle with its own understanding of God, the church, its mission, and creation, to interpret its understandings, and express them in built form. However, unless we, the various voices that gather beneath the umbrella of the Episcopal Church, share our thoughts about what we believe our buildings should say and do, we can never hope to grow in understanding and unity, or discover better ways to build. As a result, our buildings will continue to be isolated incidents of trial and error.

In 2001, a dialogue took place within the Roman Catholic Church in the United States on the question: "How Do We Seek Common Ground About Holy Ground?" The participants expressed opinions that ranged from "conservative" to "liberal," resulting in quite lively discussions. Writing in response to a particular question, one participant made a statement concerning Catholic church buildings that is worthy of people in all Christian traditions to consider:

> Catholics have worshiped in churches covering a wide range of styles. The preeminent examples of Catholic spaces throughout the ages, although quite varied in outward appearance, are likely to have several characteristics in common: indigenous to their time and place; honest expressions of the needs of the church at the time they were designed; strength

from achieving excellence in the timeless architectural principles of form, light, proportion, harmony, rhythm, tactility; well-crafted details utilizing available craftsmen and materials, and innovative use of existing and new construction technologies.[5]

If the Episcopal Church could take to heart a similar understanding and appreciation of its church buildings, then perhaps we might once again create valid places of worship.

The goal of this book is not to create an Episcopal Church of architectural designers. The goal is to encourage this church to take responsibility for creating meaningful places of worship, places that inspire, that invite and encourage prayer with God. To do this, we must learn to articulate our beliefs, understandings, and experiences of God. The words of Eliot provide a beginning, but we must find our own way to express these things and share them with others. The world hungers to experience the Divine, and our places of worship can help people find that experience. If we devote ourselves to creating places that convey our longings for God, then truly they will be places for valid prayer.

Notes

1. Paul Jeffery, *The City Churches of Sir Christopher Wren* (Rio Grande, OH: The Hambledon Press, 1996), and Pierre de la Ruffinière du Prey, *Hawksmoor's London Churches* (Chicago: The University of Chicago Press, 2000).

2. James F. White, *The Cambridge Movement: The Ecclesiologists and the Gothic Revival* (Cambridge, UK: Cambridge University Press, 1962).

3. Peter Hammond, *Liturgy and Architecture* (New York: Columbia University Press, 1961) and Peter Hammond, ed. *Towards a Church Architecture* (London: The Architectural Press, 1962).

4. In conversation with the Rev. Dr. Robert Prichard, Professor of Christianity in America at Virginia Theological Seminary, he identified at least four different trends of church building design in the Episcopal Church currently. There are those who continue embracing the neo-traditional forms of church architecture, such as those once promoted by the Cambridge Ecclesiologists of the nineteenth century. Another group maintains the architectural expressions of the liturgical movement that emerged during the twentieth century. A third group, more closely associated with evangelical parishes, is creating worship spaces that might be described as reinterpretations of the auditory church buildings of Christopher Wren—where auditorium-style seating is clustered around the central place of the Word. Finally, a fourth trend can be seen in those parishes who seek out prototypical patterns of worship from the early church and then incorporate visual forms and symbolism from other religious traditions, striving to create worship spaces and experiences that are archetypal, intentional, and inclusive.

5. Lawrence J. Madden, S.J. "Designing Space for Celebrating Eucharist" in *Initiative Report: Catholic Common Ground Initiative*, 5 (2 [June] 2001): 11–12.

A Call for Bold Leadership in
New Church Building Design
W. Brown Morton III

The Question

When is the last time you saw a newly built Episcopal Church building and said to yourself, "That is one of the most inspiring buildings I have ever seen?" If such a time has been rare for you or if you have never had that reaction, you might ask yourself why.

My work as an architectural conservator has taken me all over the world to help thoughtful people plan for the future. This planning includes deciding what existing buildings to preserve, and when to introduce bold new design into existing settings. As a result, I have come to understand something about what makes the world's great places and great buildings great. Greatness, throughout the history of architecture, has come consistently from bold innovation. Greatness has rarely resulted from timid imitation or complacency, both of which are subtle forms of cultural cowardice.

So much of recent institutional design in the Episcopal Church is uninspired, boring, and utterly predictable. Both the client and the designer appear to have lost confidence in the idea that the church's architecture can be a powerful force in spiritual development. Few building committees perceive spiritual self-confidence and innovation in new church design to an essential manifestation of prophetic leadership. Instead, we have settled for bland buildings that meet congregational needs for space and program, but which do little to help our spirits soar. We may well ask if we have become captives of today's design and construction industry. Few new church design and construction projects begin with the ambitious goal of creating a fresh vision of the New Jerusalem. Instead, we begin with "program" numbers: square-footage, heating and air-conditioning requirements, parking spaces, dollars, and timetables. We then confront the sad fact that almost all building components are prefabricated and mass-produced.

Thus, architectural design becomes largely an exercise in figuring out how to make all the pre-existing pieces fit together. Consider for a moment the tyranny of the standard 4-foot x 8-foot sheet of plywood and the eight-foot long two-by-four. Look down the eaves line of most post-World War II residential neighborhood streets and contemplate the rigid conformity that lurks behind the vinyl siding and the brick veneer. Finally, add into this the very necessary safety demands of today's building codes. There seems, at first glance, little room for genius.

Are We Afraid to Dream

Joseph Hudnut, Professor of the History of Architecture and Acting Dean of the Faculty of Architecture at Columbia University from 1926 to 1934, commented, "Architecture tells us not what men were at any period of history, but what they dreamed."[1] Are we afraid to dream? A casual survey of most mainline churches built since 1950 would suggest that we are. Lining the roadsides and anchoring the suburban intersections of post-war America are imitations (sometimes timid, sometimes aggressively over-scaled) of earlier architectural styles.

Hudnut also pointed out, "Architecture cannot be explained by social and political circumstances; it is made out of the longings and starvations which the soul has endured."[2] Have we forgotten this too? Where something non-traditional is attempted, the result all too often looks as if it was inspired by a nearby golf club, ski lodge, or motel.

Are we neglecting the important function of the church building to represent the refuge we seek in Jesus?

This is not to say that there has been no excellence in innovative church design in the United States in the last half-century. There certainly has. Regrettably, it is the exception not the rule. And I must ask why most building committees are content with a new building that is a feeble echo of an earlier style or a bland adaptation of a nearby community center?

There are three possible explanations. First, traditional church architecture feels comfortable to us and at the same time conveys an unspoken sense of past authority. Second, "modern" architecture conveys to many Christians something dauntingly secular. And third, we appear to lack confidence that our own experience of the living God is vibrant enough to fuel an authentic new expression in church building design.

The Easy Comfort of Tradition

Traditional church architecture feels comfortable to us because it is so very familiar. Many of the world's best-preserved historic buildings are religious buildings. Most of them were the result of bold and innovative design in their own eras, seeking to express some newly valued perspective of God to those who built them. We perceive them, rightly, as links to the historical traditions of faith and icons of past practice. However, we fail to appreciate that we can never recapture the past or directly participate in the faith perspective of an earlier era. We can learn from the past, but we can never duplicate it.

Our Bubble Called "Now"

We humans live each moment of our lives in a constantly moving bubble we call "now." It is always "now" for us. Yesterday was "now" when we were there. Tomorrow will be "now" for us when we get there. Now is the only moment in which anything is possible for us.

We can never remain behind in a past moment or advance prematurely into a future one. Our reality has been established by the unique interface between linear time, which we know as "chronology," and circular time, which we know as "process" or "becoming."

The ancient Greeks referred to these two kinds of time as *chronos* and *kairos*. Most of us are more familiar with *chronos* than we are with *kairos*

Chronos is linear and sequential. *Chronos* measures one thing after another. It marks a place on an unrepeating continuum, but carries no suggestion of value. *Kairos,* on the other hand, is a circular measure of time. It denotes where something is in the cosmic cycle of conception, birth, adolescence, maturity, deterioration, and death. The "something" can be a natural event, such as a season of the year or the life of a flower. *Kairos* marks a stage in the life cycle of an individual, a community, also of an idea, a political system, a technology, a theology, a liturgical practice, or an architectural style. These two very different, although always tangent, aspects of time—*chronos* and *kairos*—redefine the fingerprint of every place at every moment.

Van Gogh's Sunflowers

We human beings also "think" historically. We tend to perceive reality through the lens of our own personal experience and the collective experience of our particular community, group, or era. Since each moment is unrepeatable, by this time tomorrow, next week, or next year, we all will have moved on from this one. Our life experience and our perception of reality will have been modified by the accrual of our additional experience. September 11, 2001 is clear example of this phenomenon. We can never return to the America of September 10. Once we have seen a Van Gogh painting of sunflowers, we see sunflowers in the garden differently than before. Similarly, in terms of church architecture, because we have lived in the twentieth century, because we have wrestled with the spiritual implications of the Holocaust, Hiroshima, human travel in outer space, and now international terrorism, we can never be people for whom past styles—the Gothic, Georgian, or Greek Revival—are authentic expressions of who we actually are as Christians now.

The Traditional Versus the Modern

Since "modern" architecture conveys to many Christians something thoroughly secular, many avoid it as a solution to contemporary church building design. Present day "traditional" and "modern" architectural styles face in opposite directions—traditional styles look to the past while modern styles focus on the present or the future.

New buildings in traditional styles seek to establish a visual connection between the present moment and an historical period. Buildings imitating the Georgian style of eighteenth-century America link us to our Colonial culture and to the lofty ideals of the Revolutionary era. Georgian buildings make us feel safe, and American. Georgian churches, particularly in places such as Virginia, were icons, even in their own time, of established Anglican orderliness. The best of these churches shared a consistent and comforting design vocabulary with the fine houses of the upper class. The sturdy "Protestant" liturgical arrangement of the interiors, with emphasis on the Word and preaching, reflected the particular evangelical spirit of the times. Georgian churches were true to their own era and have worn well across the centuries. Imitating the Georgian style in new church building design is a favorite choice of many congregations. It is a safe choice, a familiar choice, and it can be a visually pleasing choice. However, it can also send the message that God is Georgian, a proposition that may sit well with some Episcopalians, but which may strike others as suffocatingly stuffy.

Starting in the second quarter of the nineteenth century, the Church of England experienced the Oxford Movement, which soon spread across the entire Anglican Communion. The Oxford Movement was a reaffirmation of the medieval heritage of the church: liturgy, vestments, and pre-Reformation architectural forms. The architectural style of choice during this period became the Gothic Revival. The feeling and appearance of many new Episcopal churches, throughout the rest of the century and well into the twentieth century, backed away from the Protestant, rational simplicity of the Georgian and Greek Revival periods and wrapped themselves in the mystery of medieval pointed arches and rood screens. As the church re-embraced early expressions of sacramental worship, elaborate altars complete with reredos, and banks of stained glass windows, took prominence again, and the pulpit moved to one side of the choir.

All this was an authentic architectural expression of a genuine liturgical phenomenon within the church that matched perfectly other artistic achievements in literature, art, and music from what we now refer to as the Romantic Period. Indeed, the two-centered Gothic arch has become a sign and symbol of "church" even more deeply imbedded in our collective memory than the golden arches of McDonalds is of fast food. And this memory is so powerful that many new churches, often ones on a modest budget, are designed with little more than a stripped-down Gothic arch in a prominent location, the hope being that this will make the structure look "churchy." Surely there are fresh contemporary design solutions that can also clearly communicate dignity and reverence.

What Could Glory Look Like?

Secularism truly has won the day if we are reduced to using paste-on architectural motifs from centuries past to express our faith. The Mexican architect Luis Barragán, who died in 1988, has been quoted as saying,

> I find it alarming that architectural publications have deleted from their pages words like Beauty, Inspiration, Magic or Bewitchment, as well as concepts like Serenity, Silence

Amazement and Intimacy. All these are nestled in my soul and though I am fully aware that I have not done them complete justice in my work, they have never ceased to be my guiding lights.[3]

Barragán designed many outstanding buildings, largely in Mexico, including churches.

We appear to lack confidence in the proposition that our own experience of the living God is sufficiently vibrant to fuel authentic, new expressions in church design. The sources of this lack of confidence are complex.

Our faltering can be traced back to the Enlightenment of the eighteenth century in Europe at which time the idea that "man is the measure of all things" finally gained precedence in the popular mind over the centuries-old belief that "God is the measure of all things." This shift in basic belief from sacramental reality to scientific reality finally tore the veil of the temple into entirely separate pieces—the sacred and the secular. Although a few brave voices in the last century, such as C. G. Jung and Thomas Merton have tried to mend this tear, we now live in a world where science mistrusts mystery. This has affected us all.

The realm of faith expression has become so compartmentalized in our daily life that we fail to understand it as a possible source for a bold new expression, through design, of the Christian gospel. We have become hostages to the contemporary meaning of the word "appropriate." Most greeting cards mailed in December say "Seasons Greetings" or "Happy Holidays."

In such a world where we gingerly pick and choose how to visually express our faith, lest we offend, it seems to be easier to stick with the tried and true rather than take the risk of delving into the mystery of our own life in Christ in search of new material. This must change. We must dare to be different. We must dare to show who we really are.

Another source of a lack of confidence in new church building design can be found in the fundamental issue of the nature of divine revelation. Some Christians feel more comfortable with a theology that suggests that God's revelation is more or less complete, having taken place in the past. Other Christians eagerly anticipate God's continuing revelation in the here and now, and in the future. Still others sit uncomfortably on the fence. For the first group, traditional church design is a clear choice. Many in the second group shrink from exploring new expressions because they do not feel competent in matters of architectural design and construction and are fearful of making a layperson's mistake.

Learning From the Kingdom Within

How can we overcome our lack of confidence in boldly seeking new expressions in church building design? Where can we begin? We can make a start by examining our own faith experience, individually and collectively, and identify the moments, events, and experiences in which faith has been most meaningful to us. We then should carefully analyze those moments, events, and experiences to identify what exactly gave them such quality. In what way may the following factors have contributed to that quality: space, volume, light, dark, temperature, humidity, sound, quiet, simplicity, richness, choice of materials, security, intimacy, awe, focal points, and views? In other words, if we believe that intentional architectural design can affect the state of our being, then the question becomes, "What can give three-dimensional space sacred qualities?" If we do not believe that design can affect our inner state, then church architecture need be no more than an exercise in "program" and numbers.

T. S. Eliot, in his *Four Quartets,* characterized the church of a long-abandoned religious community in England called Little Gidding as a place "where prayer has been valid."[4] There is the seed of a very important idea in that statement. Something about the abandoned church building at Little Gidding still communicated the spiritual work of

8

those who used it, long after they and their specific words and actions had fallen silent. The important idea is this: It is possible to intentionally design and construct sacred environments that encourage and sustain successful spiritual development. An expression from the Sufi tradition in Islam says, "The hen does not lay eggs in the market place." Nothing is wrong with a market place. It is just not the optimum locale for egg laying. What might be an optimum locale for prayer, for sacrament, for contemplation, for rejoicing? Just how can we design and construct new spaces to support vigorously our ongoing growth in God? This is the challenge.

Spiritual Euthenics

There is a fancy word for a very spiritually useful concept: euthenics. In a thin little book, *The Superior Person's Book of Words,* the author crisply identifies *euthenics* as "the science of improving the condition of humans by improving their surroundings. In contradistinction to *environmentalism,* which is the science of improving the surroundings of humans by improving the human."[5] Euthenics can be thought of as helping other people to burst into full bloom through design. Why not practice spiritual euthenics as an exercise in Christian ministry? Let us improve the spiritual condition of humans by improving their spiritual surroundings. There is no better place to start than a new church. Old wisdom will not, in every case, do. Quoting Eliot again, "...last year's words belong to last year's language / and next year's words await another voice."[6]

That voice should be bold. That voice should be strong. That voice should be ours and that voice should be faithful.

Notes

1. Joseph Hudnut, "The Gothick Universitie" *Columbia University Quarterly* vol. XXVI, no. 1 (March, 1934)

2. Ibid.

3. Luis Barragán, as quoted by Guy Trebay, "Mexico City Now," *Travel & Leisure Magazine,* January 2002, 95.

4. T.S. Eliot, "Little Gidding" in *The Complete Poems and Plays: 1909-1950* (New York: Harcourt Brace & World, Inc., 1952), 139.

5. Peter Bowler, *The Superior Person's Book of Words* (Boston: David R. Godine, 1982), 33

6. Eliot, 141.

It's Not About Us

J. Derek Harbin

I first met Bret when his fiancé brought him to church. Although he had been baptized as a child, his family never "did the church thing," so attending worship for him was an unknown. Bret had "fresh eyes." Though he was connected to our faith community, a large part of him still contained a vast resource of experience from the pagan world in which he had grown up and still worked every day.[1] One day we were talking about the Eucharist, and I casually asked him what, if anything, confused him. Bret replied, "I like the Eucharist because I experience God's mystery and I really like how you talk about Jesus, share your personal stories and struggles, and show how Jesus' words connect with my life today. But I have to tell you that when those people go up front and 'read out of that book,' (i.e., the Bible) I just 'check out' until something more interesting comes along."

Bret possesses an advanced degree and works in a highly technical field. Like many in his generation, he uses visual, electronic, and interactive sources rather than static print ones to gather most of the information he needs to function in his home and workplace. He is extremely intelligent, yet at the time was biblically illiterate. The content of the lectionary texts were as unintelligible to him as hearing "the prince found the glass slipper on the staircase and commanded that every young maiden try it on" to a person who does not know the entire Cinderella fable. Because he did not understand the fragmented content and because it was not presented in a culturally familiar way, Bret did not make the connection that the words of Scripture I shared in the sermon were the very same ones that the lectors and deacon read each Sunday morning.

Bret's confusion with worship is an experience that is not unique among his generation, those born from 1961–1981.[2] What is unusual is that he actively participates in a Christian church at all. Unlike his grandparents' generations before him,[3] the majority of whom remain active in "mainline" Christian communities, only fifteen percent of his peers have any connection to a church.[4] The gospel message is viewed as either passé or just one of the many possible viewpoints from which to choose in a growing marketplace of ideas. Even more troubling, only four out of one hundred of those younger than twenty are actively Christian.[5] By 2020, when the Episcopal Church hopes to have doubled its worship attendance, Bret's generation and those that follow will comprise roughly seventy-seven percent of the American population.[6] Those who have faithfully filled our pews in the past will have largely died away. Will we see the Episcopal Church completely marginalized with the rest of Christianity as these population shifts take place, or will we find new ways to share the gospel with these new generations?

From its very beginning, Christianity has been a migratory religion, seeking to plant the gospel at the center of whatever foreign culture its missionaries could penetrate. From the apostle Paul's work with the gentiles to Patrick's evangelization of Ireland, the church has been willing to reject comfortable, familiar forms in order to utilize local cultures, customs, and technological advances. From albs, chasubles, and basilicas to printed books, stained glass, cathedrals, and organs we have appropriated the gifts of culture and transformed them into a means of deepening our worship of God to express the gospel in ways that transformed pagans into believers.

We have not always been successful. At our worst, we have forced upon people alien cultural practices as if they are the gospel themselves. At our best we have understood the difference between the core values of our faith and these ever-changing cultural practices that express them. As Anglicans, we customarily have asserted that this core rests in the centuries of tradition passed on to us through the prayer book itself. This standard, however, is problematic because it does not take into account the fact that the ideologies of our Anglican founders, which were bound in the canonical structures and liturgical forms of the prayer book (in order to provide meaning to the unique Enlightenment worldview of their day), are no longer able to carry the same meaning in a post-modern and post-Christian world. It also is problematic because the prayer book continues to be modified substantially ("inculturated," to use words from the 1988 Lambeth Conference) to meet the unique needs of Anglican worshipers on six continents—reflecting the fact that our brothers and sisters elsewhere have already recognized that the historical, liturgical, and canonical forms, which "clothe" this core, can no longer be meaningfully imposed on local peoples.

Anglican scholars struggle to define the essence of this core, as do Roman Catholic scholars in their attempt to discern what Vatican II meant by the "immutable elements" of the Mass. Certainly the Chicago-Lambeth Quadrilateral, the Baptismal Covenant, the basic pattern for the historic shape and structure of eucharistic worship, and the work of the International Liturgical Consultation V (1995)[7] point toward it. What seems less of a struggle to me is a *methodology* for clothing this core, one that is found at the heart of the self-surrendering love of the Incarnate God:

> Let the same mind be in you that was in Christ Jesus, who, though he was in the form of God, did not regard equality with God as something to be exploited, but emptied himself, taking the form of a slave, being born in human likeness. And being found in human form, he humbled himself and became obedient to the point of death—even death on a cross. Therefore God has highly exalted him and gave him the name that is above every name, so that at the name of Jesus every

13

knee should bend, in heaven and on earth and under the earth, and every tongue should confess that Jesus Christ is Lord, to the glory of God the Father.

(Philippians 2:5–11)

In his work *The Incarnation,* St. Athanasius (Bishop of Alexandria, d. 373 A.D.) does not mince words: "That which God did not assume God did not redeem." In other words, God's action of fully embracing the world through the Incarnation of Jesus is the very means by which the Passion and Resurrection are able to redeem the world. Eastern Orthodoxy reflects this incarnational truth from the human perspective, postulating that God became one of us that we might become like him.[8] Eugene Peterson, in his paraphrase of John 1:14, writes that the Word became human flesh and "moved into the neighborhood."[9] If the Body of Christ is to reflect the self-surrendering love of God, then it seems reasonable to conclude that in order to transform and redeem, we must first fully engage the culture or "neighborhood" that surrounds us. That is to say, if the community of the baptized worship in a manner completely alien to our culture, then we cannot expect the Holy Spirit to use us productively as ministers of transformation. To put it bluntly, if we are not willing to lay down many of our familiar (but outdated) cultural preferences and practices for those not yet among us, then we are fooling ourselves to think that we are reflections of the risen Christ. But if we recognize, as Lambeth asserts, that Christ is already present in the culture, and incarnate those cultural forms in our communities and in our liturgy, then the Spirit can empower us to be a transforming new humanity, a sign of new life for the world.

In 1981, MTV premiered by showing a music video with a rather prophetic title: "Video Killed the Radio Star." Since that day, we have seen the advent of voice mail, e-mail, the Internet, cell phones, laptops, palm pilots, CDs, DVDs, and digital cable. (In today's world, one measure of literacy is knowing how to use this technology.) The print world is quickly changing to the electronic one, and the screen has changed the way we learn.[10] Television commercials change images every four seconds and live action is enhanced with computer graphics and on-line access for those who want more information or interaction. Major daily newspapers are written on a grade six reading level and are becoming more visual, appear with more color, and have web editions.[11] We have entered a world of visual spectacle where *experience,* not intellectual knowledge, is becoming the means by which we interact with our world. Some postulate that raising children in this highly visual, electronic environment is resulting in a completely different development of the brain structure, a structure in which "emotional intelligence" will be a greater indicator of success in this new world than IQ was in the old one.[12] Everything is set on speed and blur. Everything is in transition and flux. Or is it?

Last year, I attended a diocesan convention where the pressing issue of the day was whether to allow non-confirmed members to vote in annual parish meetings. During the debate before the vote, comments such as "We can't let *them* vote at *our* meetings until *they* learn how *we* think and become more like *us.* Requiring confirmation *protects us* by making sure that *they* know how Episcopalians do things." In my present role as part of a church planting team, the questions I receive from Episcopalians more often center around our use of electronic projection of visual images and prayer book texts ("How do they know that they are Episcopalians if they don't hold a prayer book?" or "How could you include that movie/song in worship?") than they do about how we strategically make connections with unchurched people. In a world changing faster than I can comprehend, I hear very few voices within our church asking, "What do they need?" I hear more asking, "What makes us comfortable?"

Despite this, the International Liturgical Consultation V (1995) was quite clear when they wrote,

> If inculturation is to be taken seriously, local culture and
> custom that are not in conflict with the gospel must be reflected
> in the liturgy, interacting with the accumulated inculturation
> of the tradition.[13]

Despite the shocking ramifications of these words, it seems that the
Consultation's work accurately reflects the gospel mandate in two
ways: 1) It challenges us to be obedient to a call, one greater than our
own personal or institutional desires, to do what must be done to
achieve God's mission, and 2) It calls us to be passionate about a few
core values and flexible on everything else. In a world where everything is changing so rapidly, principles such as these might serve as
helpful benchmarks for us in all areas of Christian life, particularly
when we are called to be good stewards of God's money as we renovate
or build new church structures that will be flexible enough to adapt to
the needs of today's world and beyond. In the final analysis they
remind us that the church's "customers" are not the parishioners, the
clergy, or even the diocese...our "customers" are those who have not
yet heard the Good News of Jesus Christ.

Churches that approach building or renovation campaigns should
not begin with a self-analysis of what they need and want. Rather they
should ask the fundamental question, "What is the church that Jesus
wants built?" (I am not referring to a building here.) As secular as it
may sound, we should begin these ventures in the same way a new
restaurant or retail store begins. We have a "product" that we want to
offer in the marketplace. How can we "market" the saving message of
Jesus in the most effective way? (And, for the purposes of this discussion, the words "evangelism" and "marketing" are, in reality, syn-
onyms.) What technology do we want to incorporate now and how can
we allow for future incorporation of technological advances? What
architectural style is the most inviting to the unchurched person in my
community, yet provides a sense of mystery and lifts up the centrality
of baptism and Eucharist? How will we, in our worship and in our

worship space, reflect both local culture and the accumulated inculturation of the Anglican tradition in our community? What will I sacrifice for those who are not yet here?

Stephen, in his speech to the Sanhedrin before his martyrdom, proclaimed that Moses was "mighty in words and deeds" because he was "instructed in the wisdom of the Egyptians" (Acts 7:22). After hearing the Apostle Paul describe his "unorthodox" ministry to the non-Jewish world, James would reply that the church should do nothing that would "make it difficult for gentiles who are turning to God" (Acts 15:19). Bret lives in my community and he lives in yours. In our worship, in our communities, and in our buildings may Moses' wisdom, Paul's passion and James' willingness to sacrifice cultural traditions be reflected in each of us.

Notes

1. Here the term "pagan" is not used pejoratively, but rather in its New Testament sense as, "one whose life is not oriented around the God of Jesus Christ.

2. "Survivors" or "Generation X."

3. "Builders" (born between 1901 and 1924) and "Silents" (born between 1925 and 1942).

4. Only 40 percent of his parents' generation are active in church ("Baby Boomers").

5. "Millenials" (born between 1982 and 2001).

6. Source for Statistics: Percept Group, Incorporated. 151 Kalmus Drive, Suite A104, Costa Mesa, CA 92626.

7. David R. Holeton, ed., *Our Thanks and Praise: The Eucharist in Anglicanism Today; Papers from the Fifth International Anglican Liturgical Conference* (Toronto: Anglican Book Centre, 1998).

8. The essential Orthodox statement describing the concept of Divination.

9. Eugene H. Peterson, *The Message: The New Testament in Contemporary Language* (Colorado Springs, CO: NavPress Publishing Group, 1993).

10. Canon Kevin Martin (Episcopal Diocese of Texas) told participants at the 2002 Kanuga Bowen Conference that the average American adult has not read a book in two years. Bill Easum, President of Easum/Bandy Associates and a speaker at the same conference, referenced his research that generations born after 1960 learn far more from visuals (including the Internet) than they do from any printed source (such as newspapers, books, or magazines). See also *Growing Up Digital,* by Dan Tapscott (New York: McGraw-Hill, 1998).

11. Our current prayer book is written on a grade fifteen reading level.

12. Daniel Goleman, *Emotional Intelligence* (New York: Bantam Books, 1995).

13. *Our Thanks and Praise,* 262.

Can We Talk about a Theology of Sacred Space?

Susan J. White

A mosque located on a Hindu pilgrimage site in North India is demolished and there is bloodshed, over nine hundred men and women killed. Aboriginal peoples in Australia and Canada take up arms in order to protect their ancestral sacred places, while right-wing nationalists bomb synagogues in the former East Germany and Serbs deface mosques in Bosnia. Ariel Sharon goes to the Holy Mount to symbolize Israeli sovereignty over the place, and a cycle of violence and retaliation ensues. Even the briefest review of the history of human conflict will disclose to us that the way we think about sacred places is of the most profound social, political and religious importance. Over and over again we find that the most complex challenges to the contemporary Christian quest for peace, justice, religious toleration, and holiness of life arise out of our willingness to defend the "sacredness" of particular bits of terrestrial geography.

The Roots of a Renewed Interest in Sacred Space

This renewed awareness of the social and political importance of sacred space is the first reason why Christians must begin to be serious about a theology of space: it confronts us every day from the outside, as a critical factor in the complex human socio-historical narrative to be decoded and understood. But there are other "internal" factors, trends within contemporary Christian theology itself, which make a theological conversation about sacred space particularly timely just now.

One such factor is the rise of creation-based theologies and spiritualities during the past thirty-five years. This renewed sense of the whole earth as somehow imbued with holiness from its inception is forcing us to ask some hard questions about what we actually mean when we talk about "holy places" in the narrower sense. In addition, this so-called "Green Theology" has led us to some serious re-thinking of certain fundamental theological issues:

- What do we mean when we talk about the "fall" and particularly the "fall of nature"?
- How do we understand the dichotomy between nature and grace?
- How were the notions of sacred geography held by pagan peoples (in the strict sense of that term) appropriated by Christianity in the early period of encounter?

To many of us within mainline post-Enlightenment Protestantism, where the impact of the material-spiritual divide has probably been most keenly felt, these kinds of hard questions about the underpinnings of our theology of space come like a breath of fresh air.

The third reason that we may be entering a fruitful time for thinking about a theology of sacred space is a counterpart to the rise of creation-based Christian theology, namely the recovery of the biblical roots of a theology of place. We have not only begun to think seriously about the creation narratives in this regard, but also the importance of things like land, Temple, and pilgrimage in the Hebrew Bible as a whole, and the ways in which those concepts were spiritualized in later Judaism.[1] Then we have had to ask about the relationship between the "locatedness" of God's saving activity as revealed in the Hebrew Scriptures on the one hand, and on the other hand, where the holiness of places fits into the economy of salvation in the New Testament. We shall return to this theme later.

The fourth way in which the contemporary mood in Christian theology provides nourishment for thinking about the nature of sacred places has to do with the beginnings of a renewal in sacramental theology among Christians of all theological stripes. How and where is God disclosing self in a new world? Are the old sacramental verities valid? Poet David Jones, who has been called the "Welsh William Blake" describes the impetus for this renewal perhaps as well as any sacramental theologian in his poem "A, a, a, Domine Deus":

I have felt for His wounds
in nozzles and containers.
I have wondered for the automatic devices.
I have tested the inane patterns
without prejudice.
I have been on my guard
not to condemn the unfamiliar.
For it is easy to miss Him
at the turning of civilization.[2]

The renewal of the understanding of the "sacredness" of places will inevitably be a part of the quest for an understanding of how God is communicating though the material in a modern industrial-technological age.

Finally, the new discussion about sacred space today is fertilized by a new seriousness about religious plurality. We have actually been talking to one another across the boundaries of faith about our respective theological worlds and theological models, recognizing that whenever we come into contact with someone else's vision it gives us the opportunity to re-evaluate our own theological position. This involves not only Christian inter- and intra-denominational conversations, but also attention to the major world religions and to tribal religions. Take, for example, the testimony of Palikapu Dedman of Hawaii, to the way in which sacred space is envisioned in his own

21

spirituality and that of his people:

> My mother and my grandmother raised me in Pele religion. We would go to the volcano to pray, and many people still do that. Go to the volcano's edge and you will see a hundred people saying prayers and leaving offerings for the Goddess. The white people can't get it, that for us Pele is all the land. She's the volcano and everything that grows there is her. The steam and vapor and lava are all parts of her body, and her family is all the forest plants and the life in the sea. You can't go shoving drills into her body like that. The old people say it will injure Pele to drill into her and to cap the steam for power, the old people say it will stop her creative force. And it will cause spiritual and psychological damage for people who worship and live with her.[3]

That kind of vision of sacred space challenges us to define and articulate how we stand within our own theological framework; how we stand in relationship to the physical world and its contents, as well as to those places which we specifically designate as "holy." How are we to talk about a specifically Christian idea of the sacredness of place?

Problems with Thinking about Sacred Space

But fertile as the ground is just now, there are real difficulties, stones in the furrows, as it were, for those who want to think rigorously about the theological status of place; most of them are related to the ways in which the theology of sacred space has been done in the past. There seem to be five categories of difficulty here.

The first is that the whole subject has not had much rigorous treatment from systematic theologians. Anglican systematic theologians provide a good example of this. A look at the recent work of David

Ford, John Macquarrie, Maurice Wiles, and Keith Ward, all of whom attempt integrated treatments of Christian theology, reveals that not one makes any reference whatsoever to sacred space. Roman Catholic theologians, even those with more particular interest in sacramental theology, also seem to have other priorities. One recent book by the French Dominican Jean Corbón is unusual in that it devotes four-and-one-half pages (out of two hundred) to the subject of sacred space. But a closer reading of these pages leaves one wondering about the rigor with which the topic is addressed. Many would want to challenge, on systematic grounds, statements like: "The church of stone or wood that we enter to share in the eternal liturgy is . . . set apart because it is a space which the resurrection has burst open." How does the resurrection "burst open" a space? And is there a particular kind of space which the resurrection has not "burst open?"[4] So the first problem is that there is little sustained systematic reflection.

Second, this lack of attention to sacred space by systematicians has meant that the discussion of sacred space has by default passed to others than theologians. Mostly the work has been done by liturgists (like Ronald Grimes from Wilfred Laurier University in Canada and J.G. Davies formerly of Birmingham University), or by people whose primary interest is the architectural history of church buildings (like Peter Hammond and Frederick Etchells) and by a few historians of religion—Mircea Eliade, for example. This has given the discussion about sacred space a certain direction and character; the interpretations of sacred space that have been proposed by liturgists and architects have tended to rely very heavily on aesthetics, on the inherent religiosity or lack-of-religiosity embedded within various architectural forms and styles and proportions. "Worship the Lord in the beauty of holiness" has most often been turned into "worship the Lord in the holiness of beauty." This has meant that most talk about sacred space has been derived from a more general theology of visual arts;[5] so the whole thing has been something of a translation exercise. One important result of this attention to aesthetics has been an almost-exclusive concentration on the "great" examples of sacred space: Durham Cathedral, the Cathedral of St. John the Divine, the abbey church at St John's, Collegeville, Minnesota, but this has ignored the very real sense of the holiness of place that people may experience in, for example, the 1961 purpose-built Episcopal church on the growing fringes of Newark.

Another difficulty resides in the fact that liturgists and historians of religion generally adopt their interpretation of sacred space from studies of how sacred spaces function in tribal religions or Eastern religious traditions, sometimes (but not always) with Christian terms interpolated here and there. Mircea Eliade is a good example.[6] In general, there has been much talk of lea-lines and mandalas, poles of the universe and aboriginal dreaming-places. Some of this is intertwined with insights from depth-psychology and semiotics, which is doubtless interesting, but should not be mistaken for Christian theology. So the first problem is that, up to now, a Christian theology of sacred space has not been very theological; and the second problem is that the Christian theology of sacred space has not been very Christian.

The third problem in contemporary Christian reflection on the meaning of place is that when we do encounter those concerned with the more specific questions of Christian theology in relation to sacred space, we find they have confined the discussion almost completely to explications of the influence of theology upon church architecture. How have the theological principles of a given time and place translated themselves into ecclesiastical buildings? Erwin Panofsky's classic treatise *Gothic Architecture and Scholastic Thought* is one very good example of studies that have related shifts in ecclesiology over the centuries to changing architectural plans.[7]

To be sure, this has been important work, and it is rooted in something very healthy that has been happening to theology at large, namely, an attention to and growing respect for non-discursive forms of theology, the sense that theology can be articulated in various modes, and in various languages. We have also begun to talk about

24

how theology might be articulated ritually/liturgically, visually, or affectively, so we find significant work being done on sacred space, in this case about church architecture, as a non-discursive way of doing theology. But this has meant that more fundamental theological issues have been pushed aside. So questions like "In what way and for what purpose does God communicate through place?" and "How is self-consciously 'sacred' space different from ordinary space?" are rarely asked in the current climate.

A fourth difficulty is a lack of historical perspective. While we have had brilliant histories of church architecture,[8] we have had very little work in historical theology to rely on. What sort of theologies of sacred space have been operative in the Christian past? It is very difficult to build a contemporary systematic theology of sacred space on sand. It is groundwork that must be done if a Christian theology of sacred space is to have any depth to it.

Finally, the theological discussions of sacred space that have taken place have generally failed to take seriously issues of justice, mission and evangelism, and social ethics. There is no longer any way of doing Christian theology of any kind as if there is not a wider world within which we operate. In the specific case of a theology of sacred space, this was brought home to me forcibly by discussions surrounding the building of the new Roman Catholic basilica in the Ivory Coast. Millions and millions of pounds were spent on this lavish, triumphalistic ecclesiastical space in the middle of a people who are, for the most part, trapped in cycles of poverty and disease, unemployment and exploitation. Can this building ever be "consecrated?" On what does the "sacredness" of this particular space rest? The social and political context of contemporary theology demands a moral edge to this discussion that has simply not been there.

Actions Make Places Sacred

But let us try to make a beginning at saying what a theology of sacred space might look like in the early twenty-first century, a theology of sacred space that takes advantage of the fertile ground and avoids the stones in the furrows as far as possible. We need to start by asking what sorts of things an adequate Christian theology of sacred space would have to take into account. What are the boundaries of such a discussion? These are, of course, the same boundaries that we would use in attempting a systematic theology of anything: the Bible, Christology, ecclesiology, and so forth. It is rather like an inter-active computer game since the choices, the moves we want to make within those boundaries, will determine where we end up. So in a sense this is an exercise in methodology, because we might want to make other (and equally valid) choices and then we will come out at a different place. That is to say that the title of this essay may infringe the "Trade Description Act" a little, since there is not just one single Christian theology of sacred space possible within the boundaries, but perhaps a whole range of responsible Christian theologies. Personally, I am inclined to begin with the Bible. And you can see already the implications of my choice of where to begin. Like Karl Barth, I am suspicious of allowing the natural world to speak for itself; it must always be read in the light of revelation. But even if you disagree with me, you will still at some point have to come to terms with Scripture and its teaching; so we might as well do it now.

There are all sorts of pitfalls when we get into the biblical material and begin to ask questions about "place," and about how the knowledge of God as Creator and Redeemer is related to place. This is because in the Hebrew Scriptures there is taking place a theological dialogue between landedness on the one hand and landlessness on the other; between being a people of "a particular place" and being a people of "no place." Theology is done out of both experiences. The God of the Promised Land is also the God of the Exile; God can be encountered in Jerusalem and in Babylon; there are historical, local visions of "the holy place" and there are apocalyptic, ahistorical visions of it, all of which are woven together into an intricate pattern of prayer, covenant, pilgrimage, belief, and promise—an overall spirituality in which "place" may have different meanings, but is never merely incidental. Hanging over all of this, of course, is the sword of idolatry. It is possible for the people of God to be as idolatrous about place as about the worship of graven images.

When we move into the New Testament material, other problems are added to those cited already, because we have to come to terms with the words and actions of Jesus of Nazareth. This is the Jesus who has nowhere to lay his head; who said that he would destroy the sacred place, the temple, and build it again in three days; who said to the Samaritan woman that there was coming a time when God would not be worshiped at the shrine on Mount Gerizim or in Jerusalem but rather "in spirit and in truth"; and this is also the Jesus who said that wherever two or three were gathered together, he would be in the midst of them. So there is an overwhelming amount of anti-placedness about the message of Jesus. Certainly, the Kingdom of God, which was the central message of his preaching, was clearly not to be identified with a place, but was describing that encounter with the living God, the fruit of which is the kind of peace and love and reconciliation which breaks down the walls of separation.

Yet, on the other hand, we get a profound impression, especially from the Gospels, of a deep concern with spatial particularity. Jesus went to this place; he taught in that place; as he was going from here to there he healed someone; he was born in Bethlehem, preached in Galilee, prayed in the Garden of Gethsemane, died on Mount Calvary, and was seen on the road to Emmaus. And it was important for the gospel writers to have remembered these places by name. But the thing to recognize is that these places are of importance not for their own intrinsic holiness; rather, they are memorable, important because Jesus was there. Even when Jesus does go to the traditional Jewish holy places, he transforms and reinterprets their meaning by his actions. (That seems to be what the turning over of the tables of the money-changers in the Temple is all about.)

The spatial particularity seen in the New Testament is not so much a statement about the holiness of certain Palestinian locales as it is a statement about the nature of the Incarnation. Tom Torrance says that the Incarnation "asserts the reality of space and time for God in the actuality of relations with us, and at the same time binds us to space and time in our relations with God."[9] Place, then, has a different status in the new economy. We might even go so far as to say that whereas the revelation of God in the Old Testament is tied to places, in the New Testament it is tied to a person and his actions, and that all of the promises tied to land in the Old Testament become fulfilled in Jesus of Nazareth. The Australian theologian Geoffrey Lilburne puts it this way:

> No longer can the community of faith hope for God to give them a special land, exclusively for their use. No longer can they expect God will unite all God's blessings of peace, security, and plenty in one physical locality. For God has concretely located those in the person and work of Jesus Christ . . . By dwelling with the human community in and through Jesus Christ, God had demonstrated that God wills to dwell in the environment of each community.[10]

This in no way undercuts the notion that all created space is a potential locus for divine revelation by virtue of its divine origins. In fact it is dependent upon it: all places partake of the christological center of creation. But when we talk about Christian sacred places in the narrower sense, as loci of explicitly Christian revelation, then the form and content of that revelation is shaped by the explicit identification of that space with the saving work of Jesus Christ.

Of course this sense of the centrality of Jesus' particular actions in particular places making God's love visible for the sanctification and reconciliation of the world will be important when talking about ecclesiology. Whatever model of the church we choose, it will be rooted in what is seen to be a carrying forward and embodiment of the work of Christ by a community of believers for the sake of the world.[11] So just as there was a necessary locatedness to the ministry of Jesus, that his life of healing, teaching, preaching, and forgiving was identified and attached to certain particular places and that those places derived their sacred significance from the action performed there, the same is true with the church. There is a necessary locatedness about its ministry as well. There are places attached to its life of healing, teaching, preaching, forgiving, and the sacred significance of those places is wholly dependent on the dominical authenticity of that ministry.

What the church has understood about its sacred places can be seen clearly in the history of the liturgical consecration of church buildings, which is really the practical expression of this idea. From the early sixth century (when the first extant rites for the consecration of church buildings are found), up to the present day, the rites revolve around and liturgically elaborate the use to which that building will be put. The whole liturgy of consecration presupposes that, wherever the people of God gather faithfully for prayer, to hear the word, for teaching, healing, and preaching, that will be a holy place by virtue of those things.[12]

To "consecrate" a church building then, two kinds of things happen. One set of liturgical elements focuses on the ways in which the building will actually function in the future. To this end, the officiant travels around the building and in the appropriate places a sermon is preached, the Eucharist celebrated, and a baptism, wedding or funeral performed (if suitable candidates can be found), and so forth. The other ritual complex revolves around the translation and deposition of relics. But even in this case it is clear that the relics' principal function is to link the present and future use of the building to the ministry of Christ. The relics serve, so to speak, as the witness and guarantor of the apostolicity of the ministry that the building will encase. Certainly it is true that as the history of church dedications and consecrations progresses, more and more liturgical elements are added. But any time ritual words and actions of consecration veer away from the idea that the sanctification of sacred space is rooted in the holy use of that space, serious debate ensues, in which words like "idolatry" are frequently thrown around.

Rival Theologies and Their Consequences

All of this has a profoundly ethical dimension, because to call a church building a "sacred space" in this sense is to demand that in its use it be an authentic sign and a witness to the love of God in a particular place; a sign and a witness that the people of God in that place are striving to be a holy people, after the model of Jesus, for the sake of a broken world. And as soon as we begin talking about "authentic signs" we are entering the realm of sacramental theology. How do we talk about the sacramental sign-value of sacred space? And what makes the sacramentality of a sacred space in any sense "valid" or "efficacious," to use older categories?

Although these issues are worthy of extended discussion, suffice it to say that we cannot any longer talk about the sacramentality of things in the way we used to do thirty or forty years ago. That is, we cannot talk about sacramentality as an isolated intrusion of divine grace into what is basically a profane world; or say that somehow grace flows through an ecclesiastical plumbing system and emerges out of the sacramental taps. The work of people like Edward Schillebeeckx, Karl Rahner, and Bernard Lonergan has shifted our thinking. Sacramentality now has to be talked about as part of the ongoing, mutual encounter between free, transcendent persons (divine and human persons) in which the physical, the material, becomes a mode of self-disclosure for both.

As an issue, this matter of sacramentality is bound up with questions about the nature of symbols and signs, and here we can include the sign-value of sacred space. What is the relationship between the symbolic significance of sacred space and the use to which that space is

30

put? Sacramental theologian Ralph Keiffer is very clear about this. He says that sacramental signs "do not actually 'speak for themselves' . . . their ability to 'speak' is derived from what people are willing or able to attribute to them . . . [for] there is a peculiar obliqueness to symbols such that they are unintelligible without reference to the community that uses them. The church's sacramental signs do not float free, but are intimately bound up with its *kerygma, koinonia,* and *diakonia*—[in other words] with its behavior."[13] So if we are going to talk about sacred space in terms of sacramentality, then in the same breath we must talk about social ethics and spirituality.

There are certainly missiological and ecumenical implications to all this. What happens when our theology of sacred space comes up against an entirely different vision? What happens when my idea, that sacredness of space is somehow related to its holy use, comes face to face with, for example, Palikapu Dedman's sense that all places are of the essence of the goddess and are to be regarded as such? Or how do we deal with the idea that some places are positively profane?

We can see the very real ecumenical consequences of this kind of clash in paradigms in a recent dispute in Poland. Early in 1984, a group of Discalced Carmelite nuns was given permission to establish a convent in a vacant theater building on the perimeter of Auschwitz. This was done at the suggestion of a charitable organization whose work involved helping churches behind the Iron Curtain and after conversations with the Polish Roman Catholic community and the Vatican. Several nuns took possession of the building in the autumn of 1984, and a search for sources of funding for its renovation began. In the various appeals for money, it was said that the convent was to be a "manifestation of a desire to pray and repent" in the face of the outrage done at Auschwitz to Jews and to others; it was to serve as a witness to the memory of the Roman Catholic martyrs who died there, and was established so that "the presence of God might be brought to a place of sacrifice and terror." A wave of protest ensued. The Jewish community all over the world was quite simply outraged. Mass actions, demonstrations and inflammatory rhetoric on both sides reached a climax when a group of United States Jews attempted to enter the building by force. Finally in 1989, the Pope was persuaded to agree to the convent being moved.

What happened was a veritable catalogue of misunderstandings, ably chronicled by Wladislaw Bartoszewski.[14] Polish anti-Semitism, Jewish anti-Polonism, the very real rhetorical and political ineptitude of officials on both sides of the debate, and two utterly divergent readings of the history of the place, all contributed to the situation. But there was something else as well which Bartoszewski does not pick up on. The Jews and the Christians involved in this controversy were operating out of two entirely different theologies of sacred space.

Clearly, for the Jewish community, Auschwitz by its very existence and by the fact that it intersected with Jewish history, and that sacrificial blood was spilled there, was place of special and status as a locus of divine revelation. (This is even true of Jews to whom Auschwitz had revealed simply that God is dead.) The Carmelites, on the other hand, coming from a tradition of the sanctification of a place by its use, thought that they could reconsecrate the ground by putting it to holy use, in this case by a ministry of continuing intercessory prayer and confession. That difference in theology was never really dealt with in the bilateral discussions; instead both sides have been left with profound feelings of resentment and bitterness, a single small example of the consequences of not taking theologies of sacred space seriously.

Undeniably, there are lots of threads left to be picked up here. We have not talked at all about the role of the human sciences (semiotics, depth-psychology, ritual studies) in shaping an adequate theology of sacred space,[15] nor about religious geography; we have not returned to aesthetics. There is also much work to be done on shifts in Anglican theology and spirituality which have helped shape the understanding of sacred space. Yet all of these are second-order issues, for anything said about such matters must be checked out against, must be in conversation with a core of a *Christian theology* (and with a deliberate emphasis on both words) of sacred space.

So what does it mean, then, to call a particular place a Christian sacred space? I originally began to think about this topic for the celebrations of the nine-hundredth anniversary of the laying of the foundation stone of Durham Cathedral, that great Romanesque monument to the persistence of the Christian faith in the north of England. So I was forced to ask myself, and eventually my audience at the cathedral festivities: "Is Durham Cathedral a sacred space?" Well, I decided that it was, but that its sacredness was not self-evident, nor was it self-perpetuating. Durham is not a Christian sacred space because the land it sits upon called out to the friends of St. Cuthbert and said, "Here I am! I'm a holy place!" nor because it sits on some ancient lea-line or place of natural spiritual energy; nor even because of its great beauty, nor the dim religious light that filters through its clerestory windows, nor even because people have been known to have had profound religious experiences there.

If Durham Cathedral is a holy place, a sacred space, it is so because it has been, is now, and (God willing) will continue to be used by faithful Christian people who are striving to live according to the gospel, who gather to hear the Word of God and to learn what it means to act upon it, who seek a ministry of reconciliation and who seek to draw the cathedral into that ministry in the name of Jesus Christ. It is a sacred space because it has aligned itself to the powerless by giving sanctuary to those in trouble. It is sacred space because all of these things together make it a valid sign, an authentic witness to the sacrificial, self-giving love of God for the world. And if ever it stops being that, if it ever becomes associated with violence, greed, injustice, pride, division, it will stop being a holy place until those things are repudiated. This is what talk about desecration is all about; that a place can become materially associated with values, actions, and attitudes that are contrary to the gospel.

This also means that the Durham Christian community, like each and every Christian community, bears a terrible responsibility for the sacredness of its space, and that every Christian community needs to be involved in the continual work of remembrance or anamnesis, keeping in mind the richness of that concept. Anamnesis is not simply a pious memory exercise, but it is the threefold enterprise of remembering, embodying, and handing on (repeating) the sacred use of the space it inhabits. This seems (as already noted) to be fully in line with modern sacramental theology that says that sacramentality is not only about God using the material to communicate self to us, to give self to us, but also about human beings using the material to give themselves to God. It is about a relationship, a mutuality of encounter, with the arrows of affinity going both ways, and the material as a medium of communication.

All of this is why the consecration of the basilica in the Ivory Coast is perhaps open to question. All of this is why the ugly concrete block worship space in Newark can be a holy place, because it is occupied by and associated with a community of Christian people who are publicly known for their acts of charity and peacemaking, and who have drawn their building into the struggle for a radical openness to the will of God. To root the holiness of Christian sacred space in anything else is to be involved either in idolatry or in magic.

Notes

1. W. Brueggemann, *The Land: Place as Gift, Promise, and Challenge in Biblical Faith* (Philadelphia: Fortress, 1977).

2. David Jones, "A, a, a, Domine Deus" in *The Sleeping Lord* (London: Faber and Faber Ltd., 1974), 9.

3. J. Mander, *In the Absence of the Sacred* (San Francisco: Sierra Club, 1991), 333.

4. Jean Corbon, *The Wellspring of Worship* (New York: Paulist, 1988), 130.

5. J. Dillenberger, *A Theology of Artistic Sensibilities* (London: SCM Press, 1987) and Jeremy Begbie, *Voicing Creation's Praise: Towards a Theology of the Arts* (Edinburgh: T&T Clark, 1998).

6. Mircea Eliade, *Symbolism, the Sacred and the Arts* (New York: Crossroad, 1986), 105–129.

7. Erwin Panofsky, *Gothic Architecture and Scholasticism* (Cleveland, Ohio: Meridian, 1957).

8. Nigel Yates, *Buildings, Faith, and Worship* (Oxford:Clarendon,1991).

9. T.F. Torrance, *Space, Time and Incarnation* (London: Oxford University Press, 1969), 107.

10. Geoffrey R. Lilburne, *A Sense of Place* (Nashville: Abingdon, 1989), 103.

11. Avery Dulles, *Models of the Church* (Garden City, NJ: Doubleday, 1974), 1–23.

12. Susan J. White, "The Consecration of Church Buildings in Seventeenth-Century Anglicanism" in *Studia Liturgica* 19:2 (1989): 197–217.

13. Ralph Keiffer, "The RCIA and Sacramental Efficacy" in *Worship* 56:4 (July 1982): 333.

14. Wladislaw T. Bartoszewski, *The Convent at Auschwitz* (London: Bowerdean, 1990).

15. A. Bultimer and D. Seamon, *The Human Experience of Place* (London: Croom Helm, 1980).

Monuments, Myths and Mission: Are These Ruins Inhabited?[1]

David Stancliffe

Church Going

Philip Larkin

Once I am sure there's nothing going on
I step inside, letting the door thud shut.
Another church: matting, seats, and stone,
And little books; sprawlings of flowers cut
For Sunday, brownish now; some brass and stuff
Up at the holy end; the small neat organ;
And a tense, musty, unignorable silence,
Brewed God knows how long. Hatless, I take off
My cycle-clips in awkward reverence,

Move forward, run my hand around the font.
From where I stand, the roof looks almost new—
Cleaned, or restored? Someone would know: I don't.
Mounting the lectern, I peruse a few
Hectoring large-scale verses, and pronounce
"Here endeth" much more loudly than I'd meant.
The echoes snigger briefly. Back at the door
I sign the book, donate an Irish sixpence,
Reflect the place was not worth stopping for.

Yet stop I did: in fact I often do,
And always end much at a loss like this,
Wondering what to look for; wondering, too,
When churches fall completely out of use
What we shall turn them into, if we shall keep
A few cathedrals chronically on show,
Their parchment, plate and pyx in locked cases,
And let the rest rent-free to rain and sheep.
Shall we avoid them as unlucky places?
Or, after dark, will dubious women come
To make their children touch a particular stone;
Pick simples for a cancer; or on some
Advised night see walking a dead one?
Power of some sort or other will go on
In games, in riddles, seemingly at random;
But superstition, like belief, must die,
And what remains when disbelief has gone?
Grass, weedy pavement, brambles, buttress, sky,

A shape less recognisable each week,
A purpose more obscure. I wonder who
Will be the last, the very last, to seek
This place for what it was; one of the crew
That tap and jot and know what rood-lofts were?
Some ruin-bibber, randy for antique,
Or Christmas-addict, counting on a whiff
Of gown-and-bands and organ-pipes and myrrh?
Or will he be my representative,

Bored, uninformed, knowing the ghostly silt
Dispersed, yet tending to this cross of ground
Through suburb scrub because it held unspilt

So long and equably what since is found
Only in separation—marriage, and birth,
And death, and thoughts of these—for whom was built
This special shell? For, though I've no idea
What this accoutered frowsty barn is worth,
It pleases me to stand in silence here;

A serious house on serious earth it is,
In whose blent air all our compulsions meet,
Are recognised, and robed as destinies.
And that much never can be obsolete,
Since someone will forever be surprising
A hunger in himself to be more serious,
And gravitating with it to this ground,
Which, he once heard, was proper to grow wise in,
If only that so many dead lie round.[2]

Philip Larkin's famous poem, "Church Going," raises the sharp question, why did the speaker of the poem stop and go inside? This, rather than the question of what we shall turn churches into when they fall completely out of use, is the one that his poem also answers and the one that interests me.

The speaker's answer is that the church is a vessel, a shell, which retains in some way a presence found nowhere else, which people will keep coming to—a shell that holds what most people are aware of only at moments of visible separation in their lives—marriage, and birth, and death—a largely unrecognized sense of solidarity and continuity with one another and of destiny or purpose. Is the church building, whether the home of a vital community or entirely disused, a historical monument, an aide-mémoire to recalling who we are and where we have come from? Or is it, by what it is and how it is and has been used and inhabited, a sacred space, a crucible—"In whose blent air all of our compulsions meet, / Are recognized, and robed as destinies"?

We have surprisingly few theological or philosophical answers to these kinds of questions, for our tradition—and indeed the Christian tradition as a whole—has felt an enormous ambivalence about sacred places and spaces. Are churches no more than shelters—crude barns to keep the rain off the gathered congregation of worshipers, like the barns in which the itinerant John Wesley so often preached, or are they intrinsically holy places, sacramentals of the presence of God among his people (Rev 21:3), which take their character from the eucharistic assembly and do not merely reflect it, as a picture might, but embody it, as an icon does?

This distinction was sharply argued over by Puritans and Laudians in the first half of the seventeenth century, but its origins go back to Judaism. When Solomon had completed the great work of building the temple which replaced the portable tabernacle as a shrine for the Ark of the presence of God among his people, he prayed: "But will God indeed dwell on the earth? Behold, heaven and the highest heaven cannot contain thee; how much less this house that I have built" (1 Kings 8:27). It was referring to this—"Yet the Most High does not dwell in houses made by human hands" (Acts 7:48)—that sealed Stephen's fate. But Stephen was only reflecting an important strand that runs through the whole biblical tradition—how to distinguish presence from containment. It is this that John makes Jesus refer to in his dialogue with the Samaritan woman at the well (Jn 4:19–24), where Jesus says that the time is coming when God would be worshiped neither at the holy place on Mount Gerizim nor in the temple in Jerusalem, but in spirit and in truth.

A misunderstanding about the relationship between presence and containment is at the heart of much confusion over the nature of sacraments—for example, of eucharistic presence. At its root lies what we believe about Christ. Do we believe that God was in Christ wholly and exclusively, so that he was not—could not—be present anywhere else? Or do we believe that the incarnation focused God's presence among us in one person, in one place and at one time in order that we in our particularity might grasp the reality of what was true of the pre-existent Word of God at all times and in all places? Sacraments like the Eucharist reflect this sense of Christ's presence, not as an exclusive container—Christ is present in the community of the church that celebrates his dying and rising as much as in the consecrated bread and wine—but as a visible and tangible focus of that presence, made particular and real. In the Eucharist, particular and real people, living incarnate lives in the real world, are fed with his body and blood and so become what they are called in baptism to be—living members of his body.

These differing ways of understanding Christ's presence are teased out in different attitudes to the consecration of churches. The medieval period, following the parallels drawn in the patristic period between the Christian church and the Jewish temple, had developed an elaborate rite, mixing elements of the funeral and baptism rites together. The church was claimed for Christ and signed with a CHI-cross; it was sprinkled with holy water, and the Christian community took possession. The altars in which the relics had been entombed were anointed; coals and incense were lit on them, and they were then dressed, and their candles lit. The Eucharist was celebrated and the Blessed Sacrament was installed in the aumbry; and finally a solemn sentence of consecration was read which set aside the church and its surrounds from all profane and common use. In essence, this is the rite which survives today and which was used at the final consecration of Portsmouth Cathedral.

By contrast, here is Henry Barrow, who wrote *A Brief Discovery of the False Church* in Fleet Prison in 1589–1590. An early Congregationalist, he had no time for such rites, and believed that church buildings were essentially idolatrous:

> These synagogues have also their battlements, and their porch adjoining to their church, not here to speak of the solemn laying the foundation; where the first stone must be laid by the hands of the bishop or his suffragan, with certain magical prayers, and holy water, and many other idolatrous rites ... Now this church thus reared up, is also thoroughly hallowed with their sprinkling water, and dedicated and baptized into the name of some special saint or angel, as to the patron and defender thereof, against all enemies, spirits, storms, tempests, etc. Yet it hath within also the holy army of saints and angels in their windows and walls, to keep it. Thus I think no doubt can be made, but that the very erections of these synagogues (whether they were by the heathens or papists) were idolatrous.

This division runs through attitudes to churches and their use from the sixteenth century to this day, and is a particular example of a wider question over the nature of sacramental reality. For Memorialists, the Eucharist is an exercise in heightened imagination, taking us back to that Upper Room, or to Emmaus, and letting us share vividly and vicariously with the disciples of Jesus their fellowship with him. Cranmer's dramatic reshaping of the eucharistic liturgy in the second Book of Edward VI in 1552 has this as its aim, introducing the Fraction and Communion into the heart of the Eucharistic Prayer itself. "O that we were there, O that we were there!" runs the refrain in the well-known English translation of the German macaronic carol, *In Dulci Jubilo,* and it sums up well that tradition of finding reality in memory and imagination, rather than in presence.

The Realists view the sacraments differently. For them, the Eucharist is an encounter with the living God in the here and now. In receiving the broken bread and common cup, worshipers experience the joy of their union with Christ and with one another, and recognize the cost of that joy—his body broken on the cross. The reality of sharing his life shapes their corporate life, and equips them to live it out in their community: the Eucharist is both image and foretaste of the heavenly banquet, of life with God in its fullness. The Memorialists' search for this kind of reality has its place historically in the search for the Jesus of history, rather than for the Christ of faith.

The contrast is explored in an interesting account of the difference between the motives of English visitors to the Holy Places, and their Russian peasant pilgrim equivalents in the nineteenth century. In his chapter in *The Sense of the Sacramental,*[3] Thomas Hummel explores the motives of the more Protestant English group through their reading of books like *The Fifth Gospel: The Land Where Jesus Lived* by J.M.P. Otts. Though the search for reassurance in the face of Biblical criticism may have played its part, the principal motive of these visitors seems to have been the desire to have the land of Jesus re-presented or called to mind (both traditional Protestant ways of conceptualizing the Eucharist) as a "Fifth Gospel." In their search for the human Jesus, the Jesus of history, many had read books like Ernest Renan's *Life of Jesus,* and the truth they were after was the discovery of and identification with the human reality of Jesus. Historical geography confirmed the Bible, and lets it speak as a sacred history or drama which reveals God and of which we are a part.

By contrast, the Russian group, mostly peasants who had saved for years and were consciously preparing for death, made a pilgrimage. They read the Holy Land through the eyes of the liturgy and their icons. Questions of history and geography did not concern them: before their eyes, the Divine Liturgy was coming to life, as they knelt in Jordan in their newly purchased shrouds, and grasped that baptism was indeed and entering into the dying of Christ, who had trampled down the gates of hell and would take them, like Adam and Eve, by the hand when they too came to die. In their ears rang the words of the liturgy:

> Today is revealed the mystery that is from all eternity. The
> Son of God becomes the Son of man, that sharing in what is
> worse, he might make me share in what is better. In times of
> old, Adam was once deceived; he sought to become God, but
> received not his desire. Now God becomes man, that he might
> make Adam God....O marvel! God is come among men: he
> who cannot be contained is contained in a womb: the timeless
> enters time.

Texts like these, Hummel points out, are all in the present tense; the
events they celebrate are not relegated to the past, and therefore accessible only through memory. The liturgy, the icons, the Holy Places are
not just windows into eternity, but doors as well; we can pass over the
threshold into eternity now. For the Russian pilgrims, the focus was
not on the past humanity of Jesus, but on his humanity and divinity
united in an eternal present. To celebrate that in Jerusalem itself was
the best preparation possible for the journey to the heavenly one.

While both groups sense the holiness of certain particular geographical locales in Palestine, in different ways, what unites them is a
rediscovery of the significance of the incarnation, which "asserts the
reality of space and time for God in the actuality of relations with us,
and at the same time binds us to space and time in our relation to
God."[4] What does this mean in a church that is suspicious of power
and presence being located in a place or person, by consecration or
ordination, as if grace could be contained, bottled or piped like gas,
but prefers to talk about a changing relationship between persons? In
what sense are consecrated buildings, or baptized persons, different
from the unconsecrated or unbaptized? In their altered relationship
both to the human community and to God, sacraments and sacramentals
bring persons, human and divine, into relationship with one another
in an encounter that changes us.

This sacrament of encounter is what Larkin is describing when he says of the church:

> A serious house on serious earth it is,
> In whose blent air all our compulsions meet,
> Are recognized, and robed as destinies.

His difficulty, and ours, is that for such sacramental signs to work, for churches to say something, there must be a known relationship between the symbolic significance of the building and the use to which that space is put. It is of the essence of such signs that they are not instantly and obviously explicit; their ability to speak to us derives from a community's continuing experience of their use.

We make enormous assumptions about what people think the sacred space of churches is for, and whether their use—even their existence—connects in any way with most people's experience and what really matters to them. "Do they still have services here?" asked a visitor to Winchester Cathedral. In Scotland, where the old cathedrals are in the care of the state, a notice is regularly posted on the door in December, saying "Notice. Bank Holiday Closing. This monument will be closed to visitors on December 25th," under which the minister has to write "Except for Divine Service." Nearer to home, a young man went into Truro Cathedral in the wake of Princess Diana's death and asked the steward if there was anywhere there where he could pray. After ten minutes of sitting alone in the nave—that was where he had been directed—he was back, asking if there was anyone there who could help him pray.

And we do not always help ourselves. In spite of our natural desire to welcome visitors and to explain the faith to them, to show them what the church is and what it does, ropes go up and the message—at an event like an ordination for example—is clearly "Service in progress: keep out." Might that not be just the moment when a visitor might see the church in use by a living community, and not just as an uninhabited museum of memories? We are in danger of locking up

45

the access to those memories and throwing away the key.

Why do people come? Both the Russian pilgrims and the English visitors to nineteenth century Palestine were in search of Jesus. What are today's visitors searching for? One reason for the large numbers that continue to visit our churches and cathedrals is to search for roots. People want to know where they came from, and the search for our ancestors gives us a place in the shifting world. People read the grave markers and monuments, and explore baptism registers and genealogies. Churches in England—especially those which escaped the most thorough Tractarian cleansing—have a layered look, with something from every period. These buildings are a palimpsest of the local community's history, and give the continuing life of the Church a truly incarnational sense of being rooted in the particularity of persons and the distinctiveness both of the locality and of the worshiping tradition. Can the visitors to our churches sense these particularities and identify with them?

A second reason is people's longing for encounter. The church is still a place to go if you want to meet people, and that is true whether you are young or old. Beneath the basic human desire for companionship lies a strong instinctive understanding that we only discover who we are in relationship to other people, and making such relationships is no easy task. Many churches receive a large number of visitors in the days just after Christmas. Is it because people's experience of their own family relationships, which ought to be so creative and life-giving, are in fact so often cramping and destructive? What kind of encounter were people looking for when they made for the churches to find someone with whom to share their sense of loss and grief after Princess Diana's death?

And third, people are looking for something that gives direction and purpose to their lives. If you go into the cathedrals of today, these great out-of-town superstores on their greenfield sites, and walk up and down the aisles—for that is what they are called—you will see people pushing their trolleys up and down, sometimes engaged in conversation, sometimes picking something off the shelves in a desultory way, but all engaged in the pursuit of today's religion. What does the church offer people who live on a diet of work, shopping, and television? If they are looking for something that makes sense of the fragmentariness of their lives, what have we to offer that will help them find meaning, purpose and fulfillment?

Larkin's "Church Going" offers a bleak view of the future. Will there one day be any more of our civilization and our faith than a barren wilderness, out of which grows from time to time mounds of rubble, which were reported to be the once great wonders of the world? Will people come to Salisbury, as they once did to Old Sarum, and before that to Stonehenge and Avebury, and walk around the heaps of rubble, wondering what it meant, and what it was for? Will the poets of the future write of the desert wastes like Larkin?

The first thing that we are offering is not desert or wasteland, but space. Space, in this sense, is ordered, not chaotic like the wilderness. Ordering space is a basic instinct, and you can see it in old and young alike. When children have no pavement to play on, they chalk out a squared grid within which they must hopscotch. Straddle the lines or step out of the charmed circle, and you are out of the game. You must keep your balance and stay within the grid. And while the English name doesn't give you much of a clue, the one used in parts of Germany does. There it is called *tempelhupfen*—temple hopping.

Because what a child is doing in chalking out a grid is making a temple, an ordered precinct set apart from the chaos of the natural world in much the same way that Romulus made a sacred precinct by driving a ploughshare round the perimeter of the land that was to become Rome. This idea of defining an area cut off from the surrounding chaos, is what the word temple means. It derives from the Greek word *temno* (I cut).

First then, the temple is a place of order and safety, a place of refuge. When a fugitive clasped the great bronze ring of Durham Cathedral's doorknocker, and claimed sanctuary, he was claiming his right to belong to another world, where mercy and penitence were linked differently. When a pilgrim made a penitential journey on his knees round the great maze on the floor of Chartres Cathedral, he was putting his life into order, even if it meant recognizing the many wrong turnings it was possible to make, and the blind alleys down which the self-willed could easily turn. Followers of the Way according to the Acts of the Apostles had a pattern to follow which involved embracing the way of Christ. But that is not all. A temple is a place of encounter, a space where polar opposites are held together in tension. This can mean conflict, and it can certainly mean a tension with no easy resolution. Making a temple is what we do when we mark out a tennis court, or set out a chessboard, where the pieces are locked in a conflict, which only play can resolve. Archetypal for the Judaeo-Christian tradition is Jacob's wrestling with the unknown assailant, who wrestled with him till day broke, and blessed him as he struggled free. And Jacob called the place Peniel saying, "For I have seen God face to face, and yet my life is preserved" (Gen 32:30). It is in Charles Wesley's wonderful hymn, *Come, O thou traveller unknown,* that the meaning of this encounter is imaginatively teased out.

But the temple is also a place where attention is focused and concentrated. When a Muslim kneels on his bordered prayer carpet, or a Japanese gardener rakes out his earth in patterns, or a student doodles shapes on his pad to focus his thoughts, they are making temples, spaces where concentration is focused, and the process proper to temples—contemplation—can begin. The rosary, that patterned aid to devotion, has its origin in a rose garden, a *hortus conclusus,* that paradise regained, planted to mark boundaries and focus attention on the mystic rose, the Blessed Virgin Mary, whose *yes* made her in Dante's words the "Rose wherein the Divine Word made itself flesh."

We are surrounded by temples, from the hearthrug to the front garden, from the computer screen to the tracery of a gothic window, from marriage rite to the diary print-out, the school timetable and the liturgical year: all are shaping the rubble of our existence, and helping us bring order out of chaos. When we come to *the* temple, the temple at Jerusalem, the same is true. That temple, which replaced the mobile tent of meeting, structured the relationship between God and his people, and gave it formal expression. In the temple, their relationship with the God who had rescued them from slavery was focused: God and his people were held together.

But at some levels, the temple failed in its purpose: while it held in tension the apparent opposites of human life and God, they were separated by the great veil, just as the clouds and thunder had kept the people of Israel at arms length on Mt. Sinai. Nor was the temple a place of order: instead of embodying the justice and mercy it stood for, it was an extortioner's bear garden. Worst of all, the temple acted not as a focus for Israel's worship of God, but as its sole and exclusive channel: "You say that Jerusalem is the place where one ought to worship," says the Samaritan woman at the well to Jesus, but to her surprise, he points beyond the particularity of space and time.

Here, as elsewhere in St. John's gospel, Jesus is picking up and expanding something that had been aired already, that the limited worship pattern of the temple was coming to an end. This conversation fills out the claim he made when cleansing the temple. In that vividly enacted parable, Jesus had not only acted to restore order to the chaos, he had also challenged the claim that the temple was a permanent witness to the separation between the human and the divine. To the Jews who asked for a sign, he said "Destroy this temple and in three days I will raise it up," and it is left to St. John to point out that he was talking not of the bricks and mortar, but of himself, the person in whom the divine and human meet face to face, with no veil to hold them apart. His claim was that in him, human and divine are one, a living and personal embodiment of God's presence and power on earth replacing the structures of Judaism.

Jesus, the new and living temple, brings order amid the chaos, holds together in his person the apparent poles of human and divine, and provides not a channel that excludes but a focus that includes and incorporates the human race into the divine life. This is the claim, that instead of a localized temple for the selected few, Jesus draws all people to himself, and so into his new and life-giving relationship with the Father. Our incorporation into the Word made flesh, the focus of the divine activity among us, not only affirms the divine potential in each person, but also excludes the notion that worship in spirit and in truth is somehow only a spiritual, interior discovery. Our relationship with God is bound up with our being Christ's, and so members one of another.

What then does the church have to offer? The church, the living temple of Christ's body, offers a welcoming embrace within a place of security, a challenging personal encounter and a transforming vision, not a narrow straitjacket.

First, a welcoming embrace. People who are searching for their roots are looking for home; they long to be welcomed back, whether like returning heroes or prodigal sons. The church does draw them, and sometimes does manage to embrace them. They write in the visitors' book comments like "peaceful" and "friendly" They wipe their feet as they come in, and even still sometimes take off their hats and lower their voices, as if they were going into the unfamiliar front room of a rather elderly relative. They want it to be home, even if they don't quite know what to do there. How do we welcome them without making them feel scrutinized, judged, and even singled out as strangers there—whether it's by asking them for money before they've even got in, or patronizing them with information they either don't want or have already?

Second, a challenging personal encounter. People who manage to get over the threshold expect to meet someone or something in church. It may be the familiar, daily encounter with the Christ on the cross or in the tabernacle. In Ascoli Piceno, the short cut from the main piazza to the vegetable market, which is held in the cloisters of what was a conventual church, is straight through the church. Many people therefore have at least a nodding acquaintance with their crucified Lord, and say

"Good morning" as they pass through. In other churches, passing through is frowned on: the cathedral at Lucca used to have a wonderful notice which said: "It is absolutely forbidden to bicycle through the cathedral"—the implication being that it is quite in order to bike in and out of the same door to say your prayers on the hoof. What we need to allow for is that people will meet God and one another in ways we cannot always predict or arrange. Paul's Walk was the name by which the nave of Old St. Paul's Cathedral in London was known, and it was a regular place to meet, and walk, and converse.

Others encounter a presentation of the faith, or are looking for a counselor, or may even find the worship of God in progress. That is when the building ought to speak loudest—when it is actually in use for what it was built for, though this is sometimes when our English habit of thinking that people in church should be allocated a place from which they do not stir does not always help a creative encounter. Finding a living community doing something, even if it is not worship, will always be the best way in, which is why vergers, chaplains, monks, stewards, and others who know what the building is for and how to express their Christian faith in worship and in living have such a creative ministry.

Third, a transforming vision. People who come to our churches long for a vision of what life might be like; they long for the potential they feel to be realized. People grieved at Princess Diana's death at least partly because they had seen in her an icon of personal transformation to which they could relate their own experience of brokenness, and their longing to be taken beyond the boundaries of their own vision had been dashed by her death. They came to church, and made their shrines; they made their own rituals where the church did not provide them. They lit 15,000 candles in York Minster, and ran them out. The church's responsibility is to give people who come to us a sense of purpose and direction.

Conclusion

In his edition of the mass on the folk-tune, *Maria zart von elder Art* by the Franco-Flemish composer of the early Renaissance, Jacob Obrecht, the editor proposes a theory. He has discovered that the mensural proportion by which the musical elements of the mass are constructed provide the same ratios as the length to height to width of the building—Cambrai Cathedral—for which it was written. Furthermore, the calendrical data give precisely the same readings for August 15, the feast of the Assumption of Our Lady. What power and presence would be generated by performing that mass, in that building, on that day; what harmonic proportions would that create and unlock?

However fanciful you may think this to be, it illustrates something of what the church buildings offer. Even when empty, they offer to the casual and untutored visitor an experience of being a "special shell." When inhabited by even one of the strands that go to make up a worshiping community's life, the language begins to form. When two or three strands are present, the chances are that one of them may resonate with those visitors. Then the visitors may be offered an icon which they can read, not just a window, but a door into heaven.

The model for the Christian life is the life of the Holy Trinity, where God's nature is disclosed for us to share: perfect love embraces, challenges, and gives purpose to our lives. Churches are there to offer not monument and memorial, but reality and relationship.

Notes

1. This essay is an edited revision of a paper read by the Rt. Rev. David Stancliffe, Bishop of Salisbury, England at a conference at Sarum College, Salisbury in November 1997. Bishop Stancliffe refers to Philip Larkin's poem "Church Going," whose theme served as a point of departure for the conference. The essay first appeared in the January/February and March/April 1999 issues of *Church Building* magazine. It is reprinted here by permission.
2. Anthony Thwaite, ed., *Philip Larkin: Collected Poems,* (New York: Farrar, Straus, Giroux, 1989) 97–98.
3. Thomas Hummel. "The Sacramentality of the Holy Land: Two Contrasting Approaches" in *The Sense of the Sacramental,* David Brown and Ann Loades, eds. (London: SPCK, 1995) 78–100.
4. T.F. Torrance. *Space, Time and Incarnation.* (London: Oxford University Press, 1969).

Highly Effective Episcopal Architecture: Integrating Architecture and Worship to Reflect a Church's Identity

Brantley W. Gasaway

erhaps church leaders and architects could benefit from a book entitled *The Seven Habits of Highly Effective Episcopal Architecture.* Like its influential inspiration, *The Seven Habits of Highly Effective People* by Stephen Covey, this essay outlines general principles by which its readers could augment the purposes and capabilities of its subject—the buildings of the Episcopal Church. This present essay will refrain, however, from attempting to comprehensively and glibly imitate Covey's book by adopting and adapting each of his recommended "habits" to the context of designing or renovating Episcopal churches. Nevertheless, the goal of *effectiveness* should serve as the primary consideration for Episcopalians as they choose how to design or renovate their church structures. Indeed, one of Covey's ideal practices—"begin with the end in mind"—holds tremendous and compelling benefits for priests, building committees, and architects; application of this principle allows a worshiping community to design and construct effective ecclesiastic architecture.[1]

To begin with the end in mind is to consciously and clearly identify the ultimate goal of one's activity and use it as the reference point and criterion by which one makes all decisions. By explicitly defining ambitions and expectations, one may better plan both the initial and intermediate steps necessary to achieve this vision. Failing to engage in this practice at the outset of an endeavor might cause one to labor intensely but fail to achieve the intended result—climbing a ladder, for example, only to discover it is leaning against the wrong wall. In the present context, naiveté in how to begin the building process creates the risk that Episcopalians will invest valuable time and resources to construct architecture adequate for some aspects of congregational life but insufficient to effectively accomplish the primary purpose for its creation. Beginning with the end in mind allows for subsequent plans and efforts to practically accomplish a specific and identifiable purpose.

The quality of effectiveness implies not only a discernable purpose, but also a standard for gauging how well this end is accomplished. To be sure, effectiveness in certain aspects of constructing ecclesiastic architecture proves necessary but not sufficient to achieving its greater purpose. For example, designing or renovating a church building must involve the habit of beginning with the end in mind through the use of blueprints and plans that guide the work towards its realization. Yet strict adherence to the construction plans neither reveals the ultimate purpose of the work nor serves as the standard by which one measures the comprehensive effectiveness of a church building. Indeed, the creation of the blueprint itself requires more crucial choices about the style and elements of the new architecture, and therefore the considerations behind these decisions point toward the purposes at hand. In assuming the task of constructing or renovating, Episcopalians must ask themselves two vital questions: for what purpose(s) have we decided to build at this time, and for what objective do we as Episcopalians and as Christians build at all?

The Purpose for Building

A multitude of factors may serve as the immediate reasons for Episcopal church leaders to commit themselves and their congregations to the complex process of constructing or renovating a church building and its space. These impetuses—growth of the congregation, problems with the present structure, dissatisfaction with the appearance or atmosphere, and so forth—provide the justification for *why* to build; they should only contribute general suggestions, however, in addressing the question of *how* to build. Too often and too easily Christians erect and esteem their architecture in light of narrowly utilitarian or aesthetic values. But does the effectiveness of an ecclesiastic building ultimately depend upon its ability to provide space for all the members, remain structurally sound, or produce an aesthetic appreciation? No, for despite the desirability of such traits, other secular forms and examples of architecture can easily meet such needs and thus prove effective for these secondary goals. Thus the present motivations for building or designing anew should naturally serve as prominent considerations but should still remain as means to the greater end of ecclesiastic architecture.

The primary purpose of a church building stems from its nature as specifically Christian. As opposed to all other forms of architecture, Christian buildings have as their end the provision of corporate space and the creation of an environment in which to worship the God revealed through the life and work of Jesus Christ. This purpose alone defines and thus distinguishes ecclesiastic architecture, and its effectiveness depends on achieving this result. In reaching specific decisions about the style, arrangements, and details of the new edifice, Episcopal leaders and architects must begin by considering this ultimate end and plan the means to accomplish it. Church buildings prove effective to the extent that they enhance and enrich the worship of the communities gathered in them, and it is with this end in mind that the planning process for a new or redesigned building should begin. As James F. White and Susan J. White state, "Worship, then, is primary in any discussion of church architecture. Every church building should be judged in terms of how well it serves the worshiping community of faith."[2] It is no coincidence that "house of worship" serves as a common synonym for a church building, for the context for worship inevitably affects its forms.

Worship, Architecture, and Identity

In no other place are the distinguishing beliefs and convictions of a community of faith more clear than in its worship. Beliefs about who God is, who humans are, and the appropriate interaction between the two—all find expression through the nature (or occasionally absence) of the liturgy, sacraments, preaching, singing, and fellowship during a service of worship. The different emphases and practices within the worship of Christian traditions reveal the distinct identities of those groups. One may apply the same description to a single ecclesiastic body such as the Episcopal Church, for it too serves as home to groups and congregations with diverse worship practices and thus identities. Because worship and architecture are inexorably connected, the architecture of each local church not only manifests but also molds the identity of its worshiping community. "Church architecture reflects both the way Christians worship and the way the building shapes worship."[3] In addition to serving as a means of self-expression, the architecture of a church building becomes a prominent medium through which the congregation proclaims its identity to others.

Thus an effective ecclesiastic building accurately reflects and communicates the identity of its congregation through furnishing the most appropriate environment and space for the particular worship of its community. Through the integration of architecture and worship, a new Episcopal church can assist in expressing what it means to be a member of that respective community of faith. Both historic and contemporary ecclesiastic architecture accomplish this task to varying degrees, for a structure may not only proclaim but also obscure the identity of its congregation by "mis-shaping" its worship. White and White recognize this spectrum: some buildings "may be a major obstacle to what the community intends in its worship. At the same time a well-designed building can be a great asset in enabling the community to worship as it desires."[4] Certainly the Episcopal Church has buildings indicative of each possibility.

58

In beginning the process of constructing or renovating an Episcopal church building, church leaders and their congregation have a unique opportunity to consider how to strengthen and reflect its identity through integrating the architecture and its worship. Many congregations have inherited structures from a previous generation that inattentively built according to traditional practices or with only fashionable or strict utilitarian ends in mind. The space and environment of the architecture may detract from or fail to complement the worship and beliefs of the community. Those churches now entering the process of construction or even renovation can start anew, however, with this goal of creating architecture that reflects and coincides with its own identity as a worshiping community within the Episcopal tradition. But should the expression of these diverse identities vary? How should a particular local church communicate in its architecture solidarity not only with its own tradition (i.e. the Episcopal Church) but also with broader Christianity?

Liturgical and Architectural Diversity

Given the universal purpose for Christian edifices, the temptation may arise to identify a specific type of church architecture as most appropriate for the task and even insist upon its applicability for all churches, regardless of tradition or denomination. Indeed, should not *Christian* worship have an accompanying and identifiable *Christian* architecture? Despite the potential attractiveness of an affirmative answer, two forms of diversity—theological and cultural—preclude any attempt to narrowly define Christian worship and therefore the style and forms to which Christian structures should conform.

With respect to theological diversity, a plurality of doctrines and practices concerning worship exist within the numerous Christian traditions, denominations, and communities. The development of such variety stems primarily from the alternative interpretations and emphases of respective groups with respect to biblical passages and church traditions regarding worship. Unlike the Jewish faith from which it emerged, Christianity lacks explicit directives within its sacred texts regarding God's expectations for particular forms of worship and its location and context. The Hebrew Scriptures contained specific instructions for not only ritualistic worship but also the nature and design of the divinely sanctioned structure—the temple—in which to perform it. It is significant to note that with the destruction of the second temple in 70 C.E., Jews ceased to continue the sacrificial worship reserved for that context, and thus Rabbinic Judaism became the dominant expression of the Judaic faith. The loss of their context for worship engendered this dramatic change in Jewish identity, highlighting the interdependency of architecture and worship.

As the early Christian communities developed, they established divergent worship practices that initially created and eventually underscored their identity apart from Judaism. Jesus himself implied this paradigmatic change concerning the place and form of worship. When asked by the Samaritan woman about the proper location for worship, Jesus answered:

> Woman, believe me, the hour is coming when you will worship the Father neither on this mountain nor in Jerusalem…the hour is coming, and is now here, when the worshipers will worship the Father in spirit and truth, for the Father seeks such as these to worship him. God is spirit, and those who worship him must worship in spirit and truth.
> (John 4:21,23–24)

Indeed other New Testament writings continue to emphasize the new nature of worship and its locale—Christians themselves "are being built up as a *spiritual* house for a holy priesthood, to offer up *spiritual* sacrifices acceptable to God through Jesus Christ" (1 Pet 2:5; cf. Rom 12:1–2). No longer is worship focused in the physical temple of Jerusalem but rather in the body of Christians themselves as the new "temple" of God (cf. 1 Cor 3:16–17, 6:19; 2 Cor 6:16; Eph 2:21). But the freedom from the ritualistic and architecturally localized worship of Judaism also allowed Christians freely and dissimilarly to interpret how and where to worship "in spirit and truth." As a result, a wide range of liturgical practices—and even the rejection of such—has developed to express the corporate worship of God through Jesus Christ. Naturally, Christians have established various contexts for these services, ranging from massive Roman Catholic cathedrals to Puritan meetinghouses.[5] The multitude of diverse possibilities for ecclesiastic architecture corresponds with the heterogeneity of Christian worship. One might say with resignation that every group does what is right in its own eyes. Nevertheless, by accepting the unique liturgical practices and styles within the Christian tradition, one may appreciate the flexibility of Christian architecture to respect and reflect different interpretations and applications concerning worship.

But even if ecumenical efforts succeeded in establishing a homogenous theology of worship, the distinct variety among different cultures would continue to produce diverse forms of Christian worship and thus architecture. In *A Brief History of Christian Worship,* James White acknowledges and even celebrates the "cultural diversity inherent in Christian worship." He states that,

> [T]heologically this [diversity] can be expressed as the witness of creation to what a lover of variety the Christian God appears to be.... It is difficult, if not impossible, to make universal statements about human societies because the varieties are so infinite. Variety also applies to such a world-wide phenomenon as the Christian worship of God.... It is indeed high tribute to Christian worship that it can be expressed in such an infinite variety of forms as to be adapted to countless cultures ranging over two millennia in time and worldwide in space.[6]

Although descriptive in nature, White's analysis implies that Christian architecture can and should vary according to culturally diverse settings. Worship practices inherently reflect not only theological identities (e.g. "We are Episcopalians") but also the cultural identity of a group (e.g. "We are Americans"). In other words, the same theological content may take differing cultural forms. Therefore the ecclesiastic structures of North America may rightly differ from those of places such as Latin America or Africa. "An infinite variety of forms" in worship allows for an infinite variety of forms in ecclesiastic buildings; one can only determine the best architecture style according to the particular worship and identity of a congregation. Thirty-five years ago Stephen Smalley came to the same conclusion as he analyzed how Anglicans should design and construct their new churches. He wrote that,

> [I]t is meaningless to suppose that there is a stereotyped shape for all church buildings at all times which can simply be imposed on any and every situation without regard to local or functional consideration...the design of a church must arise, and can only arise, from the life and convictions [i.e. the identity] of those for whom it is intended; and it must inevitably take account as well of the setting in which it takes shape.[7]

If differences in theology and culture among Christians at large produce diverse worship and architecture, the Episcopal Church must also stand prepared for similar results. As part of the Anglican community, the Episcopal Church represents a tradition built upon both the catholic and reformed heritage of Christianity. In accord with the historic doctrines of the Christian faith as expressed in the creeds of the early church, the Anglican tradition also incorporates and reflects a Protestant perspective in much of its worship and practice. Perhaps both the greatest strength and greatest challenge of the Anglican tradition has been its efforts to viably maintain its identity as the *via media,* or middle way, of Western Christianity. As a result of this attempt to balance the tension between pre- and post-Reformation Christianity, the Anglican and Episcopal Church has remained inclusive of groups and movements whose worship has primarily emphasized either the Catholic or Protestant component of the identity.

With its contemporary diversity, the Episcopal Church in America serves as an excellent microcosm for the heterogeneity of broader Christianity. Just as theological and cultural diversity within Christian worship renders the search for a uniform Christian architecture fruitless, so too does it become impractical and imprudent to argue for a definitive form of "Episcopal Church architecture." Although finding unity in the use of the Book of Common Prayer, the Episcopal Church serves as home to not only laity but also clergy with widely disparate theologies regarding liturgy, clerical roles, sacraments, and matters relevant to worship. Indeed, the differing practices within the Episcopal Church stem primarily from its theological rather than its cultural diversity. As a result, the liturgical beliefs and practices of local Episcopal congregations exist on a spectrum from conservative, low church, and evangelical to liberal, high church, and Anglo-Catholic. Although each church is Episcopal, worship styles sufficiently vary so as to demand differing architectural contexts to meet their respective needs.

Although the inability to identify a style or type of architecture appropriate for all Episcopal churches—the inability to define the Episcopal style of architecture—may at first appear as an additional burden to Episcopalians engaged in the process. The lack of objective and specific guidelines requires church leaders and architects to consider an increased number of possibilities for how they might design a structure best suited for their worship and identity. Clearly and consciously establishing the details of the end goal—an effective church building—necessitates a complex analysis of the different elements of the congregation's worship and strategic decisions regarding how architecture could enhance them.

Despite the demands of this initial stage, however, every Episcopal church will ultimately benefit from aligning the architectural plans with its identity as expressed in worship. Rather than using narrowly utilitarian, aesthetic, traditional, or fashionable guidelines, Episcopalians can begin with the correct end in mind and design a building that effectively integrates their architecture and particular liturgical practice. In order to accomplish this task, priests and congregations must examine their foundational doctrines and presuppositions concerning the nature of worship. Although unified by use of the Book of Common Prayer, Episcopalians possess differing beliefs by which they interpret and apply its liturgical directives. It is these primary convictions, therefore, that result in the differentiation in worship styles and forms. Of these beliefs, the most significant one for Episcopalians to determine is how they perceive and wish to architecturally express the sanctity or normality of their church building and worship space.

The House of God or the House of the People of God?

Perhaps the most immediate and revealing impression conveyed by ecclesiastic architecture is the degree to which the community of faith regards its church building and worship context as sacred space. In other words, the architecture of a church may contribute to a regard of the edifice and its environment as either a numinous place for reverence or an unpretentious place for familiarity. On the one hand, the design and forms of a church may implicitly declare the building to be "the house of God"—a place to encounter God, a sanctuary in which God is more present than in others; on the other hand, similarity to secular structures and nondescript features may characterize the building as "the house of the people of God"—an ordinary place in which people who happen to be Christians (and Episcopalians) meet. These two perceptions respectively represent different ecclesiologies, or interpretations of the church (ecclesia): (1) the church is primarily an institution divinely charged with facilitating the knowledge and worship of God; or (2) the church is primarily a gathering of the people of God. To be sure, descriptions of a church as either "the house of God" or "the house of the people of God" represent the extremes of the ecclesiological spectrum. Nevertheless, such a dichotomy helps to illustrate how church architecture implicitly communicates certain messages and therefore shapes the expectations for worship of those who enter its context.

Most readers will have experienced first-hand the differing architectural designs and aspects that provide these alternative impressions. This distinction results from the opposing manners in which churches address and combine three features—a large or small proportion of space to person; a dim or bright interior; and an ornamental or unadorned structure. The choices made concerning each of these issues inevitably affect the type of worship that seems appropriate within that context and determines to what extent the architecture proves effective.

Church buildings that provoke a sense of God's presence within a sacred space are customarily large, imposing structures that tend to overwhelm people through their spaciousness, verticality, or use of massive materials such as stone. Due to the initial promotion of Gothic Revival architecture by the Cambridge Camden Society (later the Ecclesiological Society),[8] most mainline Protestants—particularly Anglicans and Episcopalians—appropriated these features for their structures between the mid-nineteenth and mid-twentieth centuries. This Cambridge Movement continues to exert its influence today— not only do countless neo-gothic and related styles of church buildings stand conspicuously erect throughout American towns and cities, but also many people would still refer to this tradition of architecture as the way a church "should" look. Through aspects such as high ceilings, tall arches, long windows, supporting buttresses, lengthy rectangular naves, and deep chancels, these monumental edifices commonly dwarf not only individual worshipers but also the congregation as a whole.

In addition to external spires, towers, and steeples, the interior design intentionally draws one's attention upward to induce contemplation of divine matters. The large sense of proportion and verticality serve to suggest and symbolize the magnitude and transcendence of God; in turn, people are confronted with the corresponding impressions of God's otherness and their own finitude. Thus the worship styles within such contexts may coincide with and build upon these sentiments produced by the architectural attributes—solemnity, reverence, and ceremony most appropriately characterize the liturgy practiced within this space.

Particularly within the last forty years, alternative paradigms for ecclesiastic architecture have become more common among all types of Christians. Church buildings with smaller proportions and horizontal qualities tend to produce feelings of comfort and intimacy. Low ceilings focus one's attention forward rather than upward, and semicircular seating (or other similar designs) brings worshipers closer to both the liturgical actions and each other. Rather than inspiring feelings of awe, the architecture appears similar to other secular meeting places and affords a communal and relaxed environment; these designs accentuate the primary role of the *ecclesia* as the people of God. The architecture connotes the sense of the immanence and approachability of God—not the ruler God whose presence would dominate the atmosphere, but the servant God dwelling in the midst of God's people. By effectively incorporating these contextual impressions into their worship intentions, congregations generally *celebrate* informal, spontaneous, and collective worship.

In addition to its sense of proportion, ecclesiastic architecture communicates the relative sanctity of its space through the amount and type of its interior light. The attribution of sacredness itself depends upon its recognition as qualitatively different from secular, profane, or mundane phenomena. Churches with abundant light certainly would not indicate an environment unlike those within commonplace buildings, but a structure possessing a dimly lit interior begins to hint at the distinctiveness of its space. Likewise, synthetic light and natural light through clear-paneled windows seem ordinary and expected; light filtered through stained glass or candlelight evokes a wholly different aura. As one enters a dim church interior illuminated by stained glass, the change in light serves to demarcate the two spaces—the secular outside and (by comparison) the sanctuary within. Almost instinctively, people respond to a setting of low lighting by quieting themselves, and therefore a dim interior effectively initiates the transition from mundane to religious activity. Fostering the impression of a holy place, the darkened and hushed environment encourages people to solemnly prepare for and participate in the liturgical event. But within brighter church interiors with clear glass, people often are inclined to engage in more human interaction than humble introspection. Implying normality rather than sanctity, the abundant and familiar lighting contributes to a comfortable yet nondescript space for collective worship.

The choice of lighting may also reflect theological tenets concerning both the nature of worship and a congregation's primary perception of God. Dim and colorful lighting enhances liturgical practices that highlight the mysterious and ineffable nature of both the sacraments and God's own being. In contrast, well-lit interiors provide a sense of clarity and tend to demystify the worshiper's experience. As Tim Stafford has observed, "Natural light establishes continuity with the outside world; the Creator God is emphasized, not the God of Mystery and Revelation."[9] Thus architectural decisions concerning the amount and type of lighting affect the atmosphere and expectations for worship.

One may find a final indicator of a congregation's view of its space by examining the degree to which the structure possesses ornamental and aesthetic features. A richly decorated building reveals the high regard of a community willing to invest valuable resources in the design and forms of the architecture itself. Through embellished furnishings, detailed craftsmanship, and artistic representations, a church structure stands apart from secular settings and inspires worship through its own beauty. A religious statue, painting, mosaic, or relief may prompt reverent reflection and devotion. Most significantly, large and ornate centers of worship—altar (or table), pulpit, and font—draw attention to themselves, testifying to the prominence and authority of the institutional *ecclesia* in dispensing sacraments and truth. The space encompassing these liturgical loci serves as a sanctuary and medium of these divine-human interactions. With explicitly religious decoration and an overall aesthetic quality, these inspiring and impressive architectural contexts underscore the importance of the church's role in mediating and strengthening the worship and recognition of God's majesty.

In contrast, simple qualities and an unostentatious style may characterize a church's design. If decorative features are present, they often lack any religious reference. By intention, some congregations regularly exclude overtly Christian art in order to create a "seeker-friendly" environment that will seem familiar and thus welcoming to visitors. With their plain and modest nature, the pulpit, altar (or table), and font lack any implication of authority and instead suggest only their functional character. The absence of religious themes and architectural aesthetics that attract attention serves to place the focus not on the context of the liturgical event, but rather upon its content and participants. The space for worship almost becomes an afterthought, and therefore people tend to identify the essence of this worship more with its activities than its locale.

Thus "the house of God" and "the house of the people of God" stand as opposing views potentially embodied in the architectural designs and forms of church structures.[10] Through a combination of its proportions, lighting, and adornment, ecclesiastic architecture may provide an impression of its space as essentially a sacred, necessary context for liturgy or as principally an ordinary meeting space incidentally used for worship. But church structure exists to provide a space for worship, and effective ecclesiastic architecture will reinforce the goals and content of that worship. Therefore Episcopalians must ask themselves: "What design and forms of ecclesiastic architecture most effectively correspond with and enhance our particular liturgical practice?"

The House of God for the People of God

With a heritage both catholic and reformed, most Episcopalians will not view their church structure and its space dichotomously as either "the house of God" or "the house of the people of God." Their buildings function neither to localize narrowly the presence of God nor to shelter people only. Rather, Episcopal churches serve to gather people for liturgical events through which they uniquely encounter God in both individual and corporate acts. Stephen Smalley proposed that a building in the Anglican tradition serves as "the house of God for the people of God,"[11] and this architectural *via media* might serve as the best guiding principle applicable to all Episcopalians.

Each Episcopal community of faith faces the challenge of expressing both the sacramental role and the relational role of the church—the *ecclesia* as both institution and people. The liturgical ways in which a congregation responds to this task should also dictate the architectural means of expressing this identity. Based upon their atmosphere of worship, use of ritual, and sacramental practices, Episcopalians should determine what architectural aspects would best inspire and enhance their intended liturgical goals. Congregations should carefully consider how their decisions concerning the sense of proportion, the amount and type of lighting, and the degree of ornamentation will allow their architecture and worship to speak with one voice.

Conclusion

In a recent survey of new church buildings in California,[12] Tim Stafford observed their extensive appropriation of designs and elements from modern secular architecture; he concluded that the changing approach to ecclesiastic architecture represents a shifting theology of church.[13] Arrangements and features to promote comfortable interaction have replaced architecture that implies the authority of the church; an environment for communication and persuasion has supplanted those intended for reverential and sacramental worship; almost no religious references and aesthetic ornamentation have been included. One would never mistake these new "houses of the people of God" for a "house of God." Although he appreciates the simplicity, brightness, and egalitarian nature of the new buildings, Stafford recognizes that they have sacrificed their ability to communicate transcendence, inspire reverence, and maintain a high regard for the sacraments.

Episcopalians must not follow this trend and lose sight of the greater purpose in constructing or renovating a church building. Ecclesiastic structures should not only build a communal sense, but they should also focus the community of faith upon God and facilitate the divine-human interaction. In diverse manners that correspond to their individual worship styles, let all new Episcopal architecture communicate that the building is "the house of God for the people of God." As this essay has argued, Stafford firmly believes that "[a]ll church buildings tell stories about the people who build them and about their understanding of how God meets [God's] gathered people."[14] Through integrating their new architecture and particular worship style, Episcopalians may produce church buildings that serve as effective storytellers.

Notes

1. Stephen R. Covey, *The Seven Habits of Highly Effective People* (New York: Simon & Schuster Inc., 1989). The following paragraph summarizes Covey's description on pages 95–103.

2. James F. White and Susan J. White, *Church Architecture: Building and Renovating for Christian Worship* (Nashville: Abingdon Press, 1988), 15.

3. Ibid.

4. Ibid.

5. For a discussion of the historical relationship between worship and architecture, see James F. White, *A Brief History of Christian Worship* (Nashville: Abingdon Press, 1993), 38, 71–73, 101–103, 138–140, 174–176.

6. Ibid., 10–11.

7. Stephen Smalley, *Building for Worship: Biblical Principles in Church Design* (London: Hodder and Stoughton Limited, 1967), 14.

8. For a detailed description of the origin and efforts of this society, see James F. White, *The Cambridge Movement: The Ecclesiologists and the Gothic Revival* (Cambridge: Cambridge University Press, 1962).

9. Tim Stafford, "God is in the Blueprints," *Christianity Today* (7 September 1998): 79.

10. For the theological support and detailed practical application of each of these architectural patterns, compare E. A. Sövik, *Architecture for Worship* (Minneapolis: Augsburg Publishing House, 1973) and Michael S. Rose, *Ugly as Sin: Why They Changed Our Churches from Sacred Places to Meeting Spaces and How We Can Change Them Back Again* (Manchester, NH: Sophia Institute Press, 2001). One of the leading church architects and theorists of the last forty years, Sövik has greatly influenced the recent trends in non-traditional church designs according to "the house of the people of God" paradigm. As a Roman Catholic, Rose explicitly rejects Sövik's ideas and asserts that "the house of God" paradigm is the only true form of Christian architecture. Although neither author addresses his work specifically to Episcopalians, one

may wish to examine further the diverse biblical and traditional support used to defend the two extremes of the ecclesiological spectrum.

11. Smalley, 35.
12. Stafford, 76–82.
13. Ibid.
14. Ibid., 76.

Anglican Church Plans:
A Brief History[1]
David H. Smart

To discuss the implications of modern liturgical thought for the design of Anglican liturgical space, it is necessary to outline in broad terms how we have got from the beginnings of Anglicanism to the complex situation in which we presently find ourselves. This paper is an introduction to the history of the relationship between the shape of parish churches, their theology, and their use in the Anglican church, from the Reformation until the twentieth century. It posits the usefulness of the inheritance of the "two-room plan" as adapted by the Reformers, to the present eucharistic revisions, and reflects on the theological and ideological processes that have informed church design.

The Two-Room Plan: The Late Middle Ages

The basic late-medieval church had two liturgical rooms: the nave and the chancel. In larger churches, this was expanded somewhat if there was a need to accommodate the choir of clerics or religious, and a choir was added between the nave and the chancel. Also, in larger churches, there were often numerous small chapels, sometimes placed along the sides of the nave. These chapels were used for the reservation of the sacrament, the veneration of relics and images, and minor masses. The main Eucharist however, was celebrated at the high altar in the chancel.

Generally, the nave was unfurnished, and in any case, it was never completely covered with pews for the laity. The people simply moved around in order to try to see as much as they could of what was going on in the sanctuary. The sanctuary area and choir (if there was one) were reserved for those who were performing the acts of the liturgy on behalf of the people: the clergy and religious. Often, but not always, there were major architectural barriers between choir and sanctuary.[2]

It should not, however, be surmised that there was no lay participation in such churches, however, or that such participation was merely personalistic. The expression of Christian solidarity and community, which medieval mass attendance engendered, was unquestionably genuine. Participation in the mass was much more than the reading of pious manuals, handling beads, and holding superstitious ideas about what was going on in the sanctuary.[3] The people participated in the liturgy in ways which were complex and which had vast social implications.[4] The perception of a non-participating laity was largely the creation of the Victorian neo-Gothicism, which projected its own self-conscious pietistic preoccupations onto the medieval era, which it worshiped but sometimes dimly understood.

In any case, the two-room plan, with its division of lay and clergy space, was largely a function of the conditions of life and society in England prior to the Reformation. After the Reformation, churches could never be the same again, as society had changed when the links with the rest of Europe and Christendom had been severed, and the church had been altered when normal church government was suppressed. Yet, in excess of 10,000 buildings constructed for medieval liturgy were inherited by the English Reformed church at this time;[5] a church which, after 1549, had a radically different liturgy than that which had made the medieval nave and chancel plan so important.

Two Rooms: The Reformation

The English reformers had inherited not just new church buildings, but a church largely bereft of both the social structure and economic benefits of the church in the Middle Ages. The church itself did not benefit from the sale of church property at the Reformation; funds, even from the sale of vestments, were appropriated by the crown.[6] This made the widespread construction of new churches for the new liturgy of 1552 impossible, and for this reason, the reformers went about adapting the inherited medieval churches to the new liturgy.

The liturgy of 1552, by implication, and that of 1662, by rubric,[7] assumed that the laity would listen to the first part of the liturgy, which could be either the Morning Prayer service or the first part of the Eucharist, and that after this they would gather at the table during the eucharistic prayer.

In some places this meant that the table was placed in the sanctuary lengthwise to allow more communicants to kneel around it, and in others, it meant that the table was placed length-wise in the nave, in front of the ambo, as it was in Calvin's church in Geneva. Since the destruction of the chancel was forbidden, however,[8] it was likely the norm that the nave was used for the first part of the service, with ambo and prayer desk placed there for the readings, litany, and sermon. After this, the people entered the chancel for the Eucharist and gathered around a table placed lengthwise (with the narrow ends facing east and west) for the eucharistic prayer and communion.

This system is assumed by Hooker, who states that Anglicans do this not to maintain popery, nor to symbolize the Jewish temple, but as a function of the practical needs of the liturgy.[9] By Hooker's period, the Anglican synthesis of modern liturgy and medieval building was so complete that Hooker neglected to mention the fact that the two-room plan was an inheritance from the popish church. Indeed, he argues that it is the most perfect fulfillment of Anglican liturgical needs and Protestant ideals of non-clericalism.

Thus the medieval and Protestant were welded together as the people entered the sanctuary and the whole church building became inhabited by the entire *ecclesia*. The building, once neatly divided, became a landscape which the clergy and laity traversed in motions set to the rhythms of the eucharistic liturgy. The Caroline Divines and baroque architects like Christopher Wren and Nicholas Hawksmoor built upon this model to develop a distinctly Anglican synthesis.

Two Rooms: The Renaissance and Baroque

After the death of Elizabeth in 1603, the accession of the Scot, James Stuart, and the peace with Spain, the religious and social situation which had given birth to the two-room synthesis changed. After half a century of alienation from Catholic Europe, England re-entered the continental scene. Prior to this period, everything that had been Catholic and continental had been seen as trappings of the foreign states that wished to de-stabilize the English kingdom and church. With the Spanish peace, England was faced with the challenge of legitimizing its polity, including the church, in a Europe which included states which were, on the whole, much more artistically and theologically sophisticated.

The Canons of 1604 established the need for decoration in church, the placement of the Ten Commandments in the chancel, the handsome ambo, the place of the people, and the font at the back of the church.[10] The prayer book of 1662 allowed for the use of a choir to sing an anthem, and added some manual acts to heighten the theology and visual character of the eucharistic liturgy.[11]

The two-room plan continued to dominate, and the practice of the movement of people into the sanctuary became an expression of a high eucharistic theology. Travelers to the Near East compared the liturgy of the Orthodox churches to the Anglican liturgy.[12] The early church fathers were translated into English[13] and it was believed that the practice of the apostles, that of the Constantinian church, and the Anglican liturgy were very similar in character.[14] These observations tended to increase the self-confidence of Anglican theologues who believed that their church was not merely an invention of the sixteenth century, but an ancient and catholic one.

The movement into the sanctuary became laden with symbolic meaning. The first purpose-built Anglican churches used the two-room plan as their model, although the sanctuary was widened to more suitably serve its purpose as a place for the communicant. On the whole, such buildings were much more ornate than medieval parish churches adapted for Protestant worship. The choir remained either a fluid, moving group that situated itself in front of the people during the singing of anthems or, after 1660, in a choir loft at the back of the church.

This was an exciting period in the development of Anglican churches. The Protestant liturgy was shown to have recovered serious patristic and ecumenical principles. An Anglican architecture based upon ancient, modern, and ecumenical principles, and most importantly, the needs of Anglican liturgy, arose and garnered widespread acceptance and some international acclaim. There were, however, some important objections to the developments.

Puritans wished to remain in their pews and not to have to come forward to receive communion. They also opposed the two-room plan, partly because they couldn't see or hear the altar prayers from their pews.[15] Puritans had also carried out intensive, but not extensive, programs of iconoclasm, thus expressing resistance to the Stuart effort to give the Anglican liturgy a rich, Catholic character.[16] Generally speaking however, these Calvinist impulses were not very influential upon Anglican church planning.

One Room: Whig Neo-Classicism

At the beginning of the eighteenth century, the Whig majority in the House of Commons, the end of the Stuart dynasty, and the rise of the middle class coincided with a reaction against baroque flamboyance in English art and society. There was a new interest in the round church, in which all could see the pulpit and chancel from their places and, more importantly, everyone could see everyone else, at least from the gallery.

The idea of the round church had its fundamental expression in the plan put forward by Jeremy Bentham in his book *Panopticon.* In this work, he described the way that a single-room building could be a tool of surveillance. The inmates of such a building had their rights secured by the fact that it was impossible to do anything in secret, and the entire space was equally surveyable by all.

The linear, processional two-room building had been the basis of Anglican liturgical planning. The idea of being in one place and then moving into another had exegeted the liturgy, and had reinforced the idea that liturgy was something which involved congregational movement, as well as auditory and visual experience. The one-room plan froze the congregation in their place, and gave all an equal view of the building and the other members of the congregation. In this sense, it reinforced the Whiggish, republican, and anti-hierarchical values which were dominant at the time.

Throughout this period, the ambo, the altar, and the prayer desk became increasingly centralized at the front of the church in order to expedite the visual character of the rites. It has been said that the round church was the quintessential auditory church, but this is not necessarily affirmed by the legacy of early eighteenth-century music and preaching.

Two Rooms: Hanoverian Romanticism

Although the round or central church was perhaps the most dramatic and unique expression of neo-classicism, there were parallel currents in church design running through the period. The two-room plan continued to exert influence, and its ultimate justification was a century and a half of Anglican liturgical practice. Interest in church decoration, particularly of the chancel, was renewed by the Royal Academy in 1773 when it attempted, under the leadership of Sir Joshua Reynolds, to have the doctrine of the Church of England concerning worship changed to allow for more artistically rich churches.

A substantial and powerful high church movement began the Hanoverian period, and led to the largest single Anglican church building program in history, the Million Pound Fund Commission of 1818, which oversaw the building of six hundred new churches. This period saw the re-instatement of the two-room church, the requirement that the ambo be placed where it would not obstruct the view of the altar, and renewal of interest in primitive and medieval church design.[17] The die seems to have been cast in the eighteenth century, however, which had locked the congregation into their pews during all of the liturgy except at the moment of receiving communion.

Two Rooms: Neo-Gothic to Arts and Crafts

The one artistic movement that all Anglicans believe that they understand is the neo-Gothic. Indeed, most Anglican places of worship bear some evidence of the influence of the Gothic revival. In the late eighteenth century, architects, for a vast range of reasons still debated by historians, started to emulate the models of the Middle Ages. At first, this emulation took the form of a playful emphasis on the Gothic elements that had existed in baroque architecture.[18] The Gothic tendency slowly became more archaeological, eventually manifesting itself in the codification of medieval forms by the Cambridge Camden Society.

In the Gothic period, there was a self-conscious attempt to evoke the emotions of awe and mystery that Victorians felt in medieval churches. There was also a belief that the medieval architect had created these effects by fair and wholesome means, rather than through deliberate dramatic tricks which had been popular in baroque architecture.[19] This preoccupation with the existence of architectural "honesty" or "genuineness" continued through the modern period.

The main result of the neo-Gothic period was the idea that there was something profoundly and incontrovertibly English about medieval architecture. The fact that older versions of the same style of buildings were visible in Spain, Germany, and France did not inhibit this sense of nationalism.[20]

The two-room plan, with the choir situated between the nave and the people, the place of the religious in medieval churches, became the norm. This removed the table from the people, who had once gathered around it in the chancel. The re-introduction of the chancel screen, which was not an obstacle to liturgical participation when the people entered the choir for communion, had the effect of further emphasizing this clergy-laity division. The people remained in their place, except to come forward to receive communion. The pulpit thus permanently took its place off to one side of the church, as a central pulpit made it impossible for a congregation permanently placed in the nave to see the altar. This is the manner in which most Anglican churches are still arranged and used.

The positive effects of the neo-Gothic movement upon the liturgy cannot be read purely in terms of its function in worship. The placement of the choir at the front of the church may have had a positive effect on congregational singing. The medieval style at least opened the possibility that a rich ceremonial landscape such as that of the medieval church might be recovered. Finally, the neo-Gothic had an immense effect on the self-consciousness of Anglicans—that they belonged to a single, culturally English communion. It was exported all over the empire, although its most enthusiastic proponent, the Cambridge Camden Society, suggested that primitive and colonial cultures start with a more simple "hyperborean" or "speluncar" version of the Norman style and evolve towards the Gothic, lest they make the mistake of seeing themselves as having attained to the same state of social and religious development as the mother nation.[21]

The Basilica and the Round Church: Modernism

In the early Edwardian period, the Arts and Crafts movement led a reaction against the antiquarianism of neo-Gothic and arbitrary styles in general in favor of modes of construction based upon structural and practical needs. It was hoped that such an approach would re-ground ecclesiastical architecture in the most fundamental principles of the church, which were poverty and genuineness.[22]

In the Anglican church, these principles were not so generally applied to liturgical practice as they were to church architecture. For this reason, the majority of modernist Anglican churches from the thirties and forties are functionalist and structuralist buildings planned and furnished for neo-Gothic liturgy. After the Second World War, however, this changed, and the two most important models became the round church and the basilica.

The implications of the round church had not really changed since the eighteenth century. It was a symbol of a community which was non-hierarchical, in which everyone could see everyone else and the actions of the liturgy without having to move from their pews, which, by the nineteenth century, had become the compulsory, static place of the worshipper. It had a peculiar resonance in a century in which cultural, racial, and religious communities militantly defined themselves against other communities, and surveillance became the means by which societies exerted their power and influence on their members. On the other hand, the round church appealed to the highly realized eschatology of late twentieth-century liturgical texts, and to the therapeutic values of a communitarian ecclesiology. Round modernist churches are therefore important exercises in religious art, insofar as they are artistic expressions of values that were contemporary to their construction.

The second important model was the basilica. Aided by the rediscovery of the importance of ancient liturgical texts and by the primitivism

81

of writers such as Dom Gregory Dix, who believed, as did the Anglican Primitive Christians of the seventeenth century, that the arrangement of the furniture in Constantinian Basilicas was based on that of apostolic house churches,[23] a great revival of certain patristic features took place. The most influential feature of the revival was the placement of the presider behind the table. Sometimes the presider's chair itself was placed behind the table and the assistants flanked the presider. The overall effect of this development was to bring the presider into visual contact with the people. Visual contact had been lost during the Oxford Movement, when the presider began to stand at the west side of the altar and face away from the people, instead of standing at the north end as directed by the rubrics of the prayer book. This was theologically significant in that it emphasized that the presider was a member of the assembly.

The difficulty with the practice is that few Anglican chancels could easily be accommodated to this program, unless the table was placed in the crossing where it is difficult for most of the congregation to see. Also, the placement of the presider's chair above and behind the table put the presider in the place that the altar, a symbol of God's presence among his people, had formerly occupied. This sometimes gives the undesired impression that the cleric has a higher theological position in the liturgy than is generally supported by Anglican theology. Although this was somewhat countered by practices such as the movement of the clergy down among the people for the homily, or by the use of a moveable lectern placed close to the people, the patristic model, especially when forced upon the neo-Gothic plan, had more difficulties than could easily be resolved through moving of furniture.

The congregation basically remained static, and the liturgical reforms focused on giving the clergy more space, while the people remained pent up in pews, suffering the ambulatory and visual ennui which had been their lot since the middle of the eighteenth century.

Dynamic Use of Space: The Once and Future Anglican Liturgical Space

The appropriation of space for worship happens every Sunday in every church in the world. Therefore, it is not surprising that, even when there are difficulties in general practice, some places continue to experiment with their worship environments. Although for this reason it is impossible to make sweeping comments on everything creative and useful that is happening, there are a few specific developments of widespread interest.

The most interesting development has been the re-appropriation of the Anglican principle of movement of the congregation from the part of the church where the Word is celebrated to the part of the church where the Eucharist is celebrated. This practice has been revived in parish churches from Africa to California, in English Gothic cathedrals, baroque churches, and rural church halls. Its rationale has been found in sources as diverse as Hooker, Syrian liturgy, local culture, and modern dance. Besides requiring the removal of some furniture from the chancel in order to accommodate the people, it seems not to impose great spatial requirements upon the architecture.

There is a general movement in the world of architecture that seeks to reconsider the value of classical tradition and the ancient forms and principles. This is of significance to church design because modernism reacted strongly against the use of historical architectural forms and precedents, electing to establish its own criteria for church building. We are now therefore faced with the possibilities of re-appropriating parts of the tradition for study and for possible renewal and use. The classical Anglican usage of the late seventeenth century, in which two rooms were utilized along with linear movement of the whole congregation, seems to be one aspect of our Anglican heritage which is particularly worthy of consideration for this purpose.

Of course, the issue of liturgical space is more vast than the issues of eucharistic celebration alone. It was quite clear at the Fifth International Anglican Liturgical Consultation, in Dublin in 1995, that baptismal space and space for the offices were almost equal in stature to eucharistic space in the minds of many members. Issues of decoration, multi-purpose space, sacrality, consecration, and so on were also of importance, and intrinsic to the theology and form of church buildings. Behind the discussion of such complexities, however, there was the general realization that the form of the liturgy is precedent to its architectural and artistic landscape. This has not always been universally recognized, and the reality is that from the beginning of the history of the liturgy there has been both liturgical imperative and the adaptation of the liturgy to pre-existent architecture and art. We are faced with the challenge, however, of constantly going back to the liturgy's structure, and to its basic theological tenets, and checking our practice against these. In the end, we will inevitably find that some inheritances are more useful and more closely match the reigning ecclesiology and structure of the liturgy than others. This process must, therefore, be ongoing, and should engage more of our study and energy than it has done so far. The study of the history and development of church plans in the Anglican era is an intrinsic part of this process.

Notes

1. This essay is excerpted from *Our Thanks and Praise: The Eucharist in Anglicanism Today,* David R. Holeton, ed., (Toronto: The Anglican Book Centre, 1998),174–184. Used with permission.
2. See Eamon Duffy, *The Stripping of the Altars* (Princeton: Yale University Press, 1992), 472ff.
3. Miri Rubin, *Corpus Christi: The Eucharist in the Late Middle Ages* (Cambridge: Cambridge University Press, 1994), 98–108, 147–162.
4. Duffy, 109ff.
5. John Martin Schnorrenberg, *Early Anglican Church Architecture, 1558–1662, Its Theological Implications and its Relation to the Continental Background* (unpublished Ph.D. Thesis, 1946), appendix 1.

6. H.B. Walters, ed., *London Churches at the Reformation, with an Account of their Contents* (London, 1939), 1–10.

7. F.E. Brightman, ed., *The English Rite* (London, 1921), 2:677.

8. Ibid., 1:127.

9. Richard Hooker, *Lawes* V, xv, 9.

10. John Henry Blunt, *The Book of Church Law* (Oxford, 1872), 400ff.

11. Brithman, 1:149; 2:693.

12. See George Wheler, *A Journey into Greece* (London, 1682).

13. William Whiston, *Primitive Christianity Reviv'd* (London, 1711), Vv. III–IV.

14. See, for example, Joseph Mede, *Churches, that is, Appropriate Places for Christian Worship: Both in, and since the Apostles' Times* (London, 1638).

15. "The Westminster Directory," *Liturgies of the Western Church*, ed. Bard Thompson (New York: Meridian, 1962), 369.

16. *Commons Journal* 2:35, 278–79.

17. Michael H. Port, *Six Hundred New Churches* (London, 1962), 61.

18. See Sir Joshua Reynolds, *Fifteen Discourses* (London, 1789) XII, Dec. 11, 1786.

19. John Augustus Welby Pugin, *Contrasts* (London, 1841), 35.

20. A development that can be traced to the work of Thomas Rickman, *An Attempt to Discriminate the Styles of English Architecture in England from the Conquest to the Reformation* (London, 1819), and continuing through Pugin and Ecclesiology until Ninian Comper rebelled against it late in his career.

21. Anon., "Colonial Church Architecture in Ceylon," *Ecclesiologist* 7 (1847): 161–71; William Scott, "Some Notes on the Cathedral of Las Palmas with a Few Thoughts on Tropical Architecture," *Ecclesiologist* 12 (1851): 29–45. For references to hyperborean architecture see Ecclesiologist Letters (mainly anonymous) 7 (1846) 190–193; 8 (1877) 63; W.S. Scott, ibid. 12 (1851), 400.

22. Peter Hammond, *Liturgy and Architecture* (London: Barrie and Rockcliff, 1960), Introduction.

23. Dom Gregory Dix, *The Shape of the Liturgy* (London: Seabury, 1945), 143.

A House for the Church That Sings[1]
Carol Doran

B oth architecture and music are arts. The architect arranges materials in space for the design and erection of buildings; the musician arranges sounds in time to produce "a continuous, unified, and evocative composition, as through melody, harmony, rhythm, and timbre."[2] By accepting and respecting one another's understanding of art's role in enhancing the church's worship, artists working in space and sound can find harmonious new ways to further the church's mission in the world.

Leaders of Episcopal churches and schools who have known this collaboration in sweet reality do not claim this process is easy. In most cases, years of dreaming, talking, planning, seeking support, negotiating patiently and careful oversight have accompanied renovation or building projects. The experience of people who have been through this process can inform our own hopes for physical changes, making possible a more deeply prayerful liturgical life for our congregations.

The scope of this essay will allow little more than an introduction of basic principles. It is my hope that this summary will lead to further study, continuing discussion, and prayerful planning of the environment in which we worship.

Communication

Ours is not the first generation to consider the benefits of planning physical space to enhance communication of the sounds of prayer, both spoken and sung. First-century meeting synagogues often had raised wooden platforms for worship leaders, presumably, to allow them to be better seen and heard.[3] Rows of benches facing one another in monastic communities over many centuries have allowed optimum communication as two groups take turns singing verses of the Psalter.

Our present Book of Common Prayer implies that the physical arrangements that facilitate the exchange of sights and sounds among faithful people gathered to worship are crucial. Hymns and other musical settings are expected to be sung by all the gathered assembly.[4] People feel encouraged to take their parts most effectively when they can hear and be supported by the sounds of other voices, and when the one(s) providing instrumental accompaniment and leadership can hear them all.

This also is true for the congregation's participation in spoken texts. Nearly every liturgy in our prayer book invites people to pray the Lord's Prayer together and many include a creed to be said aloud by all the people.[5] The rites expect people to hear and to answer the celebrant's words: "The peace of the Lord be always with you," "Alleluia, Christ is risen," and numerous other biddings.

As congregations strive for renewal of worship, greater integrity is realized when people are encouraged to respond aloud to one another. Increased visual and sensate connectedness is essential if continuing revitalization of liturgical prayer is to be encouraged over a period of time. When faithful people are able to see and hear not only the leaders, but also others in the gathered congregation, their own part in the liturgy is more likely to be a genuine response, affected by what they see and hear in others, rather than simply words read from a book or a service sheet.

Several forms for "The Prayers of the People" invite the offering of prayers in the midst of the congregation.[6] Praying silently is done, of course, but when someone prays aloud in the midst of others, it is probably spoken with the expectation that others will hear and join in offering that same petition or thanksgiving. The acoustical situation that allows people to hear one another not only encourages their prayer, but also offers essential information for the task. Who, but the most courageous, would offer a petition aloud, if there were a chance that someone whose words they could not hear or understand may have just prayed for the same concern?

History Forms Us Still

One of the great treasures of the Anglican tradition is the English cathedral. These (usually) noble structures stand as symbols of religious imagination and inspiration, and of faith's ability to survive war, pestilence and budget cutting. We enjoy televised images of elegant ceremonies taking place in them. We love to visit them and hang pictures of them on our walls.

Our admiration of all a cathedral represents, however, can sometimes influence our vision for the life of our own congregations. Beauty, vitality, and an atmosphere of reverence are appropriate for every worship space, but like clothing for the body, the building for the church should fit the needs of the local body of Christ. A large building is needed to accommodate a large group; a large building can sometimes become a burden to a small group.

More than suitable size is implied here. The church's gathering space must be appropriate for the activities of that body. Medieval cathedrals served the church as symbols of ecclesiastical wealth and power and they also functioned regularly as civic gathering places. Few congregations today design or renovate a building with either of those functions in mind. But committees planning worship space sometimes cherish a "cathedral concept" at a level of consciousness of which they are unaware. Marion Hatchett reminds us that from the mid-nineteenth century, the medieval Gothic church has been "accepted as the ideal, and the building began to determine the worship rather than the worship determining the setting."[7]

Worship space that provides only an opportunity to "be" in a beautiful place is inadequate for our time and our church. Gracious means of reciprocal communication are essential if the faithful are to have the integrity of prayer so deeply desired in our time. The critical and simple questions inherent in all architectural and liturgical planning arise here: "Why are we doing this (this gathering, this ritual prayer and song, this going forth to serve)?" and "What architectural choices are implied by our genuine intention?"

The space should permit our gathering, our praying and singing, and should provide places in the building where we might be in small groups to learn, to grow spiritually, and to equip ourselves for service in the world. History offers us many worship spaces that are beautiful and inspiring, but we are not called thoughtlessly to mimic its examples.

The Sounds of Prayer

SPOKEN AND SUNG PRAYER

Churches must be acoustically beneficial for sounds both spoken and sung. These two kinds of sound are actually part of the same spectrum, and the ability of the nearly imperceptible crossing from speaking to singing to enhance the presentation of sacred texts has been known in religious ritual for centuries.[8]

This expressive range of sound often is heard when a preacher's spoken words gradually slip into not only rhythmic pattern, but also into a vocal sound of vibratory regularity, which is recognized as chanting or singing. Some African-American traditions recognize this as the sermon's summary "whooping." The increased energy driving the preacher's voice causes it to ring through the space and to draw the minds and bodies of the listeners into the climactic close of the sermon.

SHAPE AND SIZE OF SPACE

Early in the project, the church building committee should require that the architect's services include the consultation of an experienced acoustical consultant. Those who suggest that such professional services are a luxury "for a church of our size," might be encouraged to reflect on the relative costs of construction necessary to correct unsatisfactory acoustics that might occur without such advice.

While acoustics, "the scientific study of sound, especially of its generation, transmission, and reception,"[9] are beyond the expertise most of us can claim, it is important for us to respect what others know about it. Acknowledging the part that acoustics will play in the "successful" or "disappointing" outcome of a project should encourage us to understand all that we can as we make plans for large and small projects.

If the person, expert in acoustics, is not also knowledgeable and concerned about liturgical practice, clergy, musicians and committee members can take responsibility for bringing these matters into discussions whenever required. The full range of concerns must be dealt with all along the way; talking about the means to be certain the presider is heard, as well as seen, cannot wait until "later."

Jack M. Bethards has written a succinct summary of principles of acoustical planning which could serve well as a launching pad for discussion and further study. In an article aptly titled, "Don't give up on Acoustics," he writes about factors essential to "a good acoustic."[10]

1. "A building is good when the musical sounds produced are transmitted to all of the listeners (including the musicians themselves) with clarity, beauty and warmth. First, the bass tones and the treble tones must be received just as they are generated by the organ or singer. Second, there must be a sufficient period of reverberation so that the sound does not end abruptly."[11]

2. "Reverberation ('persistence of sound in a room after the source has stopped'[12]) is what eliminates harshness and dullness, and substitutes in their place warmth and beauty."[13] Two factors are of critical importance in reverberation:

Shape of the space. Both "free air space above for sound to develop" and "close enough [to the people] reflective surfaces to direct it" are necessary. (For instance, a space with low ceilings would not provide these essential qualities.)

Materials of which the building is constructed should meet two requirements: they must be "solid and reflective."[14] Materials like stone, brick, concrete block, thick plaster or well-supported, double-thickness, gypsum wallboard encourage reflection of sound waves. Surfaces that "vibrate" (acoustically absorbent ceiling panels or fabric) "move with the sound waves and cancel them."[15]

3. "The floor is the most important surface because it is closest to the people."[16] Hardwood, stone, clay or resilient tile are good choices for this surface, with the possible use of a dampening material such as thin, hard carpeting in places where people walk. In any case, thick carpeting, particularly with a padding, is "absolutely out."[17]

Other factors to be taken into consideration when planning worship space include: a quiet background (freedom from intruding noises like noisy fans from heating and air conditioning systems or sounds that seep through thin walls) and sound that is distributed evenly (no "dead" pockets where people cannot hear).

Visiting existing buildings and talking frankly with those who worship in them can reveal much that is important. A gentle question such as, "What would you do differently if you were to begin this project again tomorrow?" can result in useful counsel for your own planning.

These and other fundamental principles of acoustical planning are explained in greater detail in books and articles listed in the resource bibliography found in the appendix of this book. They contain information that will both amaze and prepare members of the church building committee to work responsibly with an acoustical consultant.

NATURAL AND ELECTRONIC AMPLIFICATION

All spaces used for worship need those qualities that equip it to receive and amplify the full range of sounds present in both speaking and singing. This goal is frustrated when the space is too large or too small (particularly when the ceiling is too low) or when wall surfaces are either too sound absorbent or reflect sound too loudly or too harshly. Careful acoustical design seeks the *natural amplification,* which is part of reverberation in a carefully planned space.

Electronic amplification, functionally, is far less effective or dependable than good fundamental architectural design, which incorporates acoustical considerations. This fact alone should encourage church building committees to choose to use electronic amplification only when physical properties of a room cannot be arranged to maximize natural sound. This would include situations in which the space is so large or of such a shape that people in parts of the room cannot hear or understand the spoken word. (Generally speaking, a maximum of sixty feet between presenter and listener is optimally effective for natural sight and sound communication.)

Assuming that expensive amplification systems are integral to worship sidesteps the critical question, "Why are we doing this?" The response, "Because everyone else does it," has little value for the long term.

If a very large space is needed for the gathering, and if it is impossible to reorient seating in the space to bring more people closer to the liturgical center (by rotating the axis of the room, for example), then microphones and amplification are better than people not hearing at all. And of course, a sound system that aids in carrying sound to those with limited hearing is a positive addition to the life of the community. Any amplification system considered for purchase should be of excellent quality and, preferably, designed with the help of an experienced acoustical consultant. One salesperson's opinion should not be considered an adequate basis for such a substantial investment. An "acoustical engineer" is not the same as an experienced acoustical consultant.

And while electronic amplification has proven itself useful when inexperienced singers or readers are leading worship, in general, the assumption that amplification will compensate for the loss of natural overtones and the absence of "blending" in voices singing together simply cannot be supported. When carpeting or lack of informed planning causes a loss of natural acoustic beauty, electronically amplifying what is left behind will not make it beautiful.

The question of visual clutter also should be considered seriously when planning acoustical arrangements. Some people consider the presence of cables, microphones, mixing boards, microphone stands and speakers of all sizes a normal part of music making in large groups, but not everyone agrees. The congregation, which seeks to know God's presence more fully in worship, must ask the same simple questions of every aspect of its corporate prayer, including the appearance of its worship space: "Why are we doing this?" "What choices are implied by our genuine intention?" When the negative effects of the supporting equipment required for the presumed benefit exceeds that presumed benefit, the group may want to consider whether it still remains a viable choice. "Is the price too high?"

There can be no "rule" here; clergy, musicians, and worship committees must consider these questions in light of their local situations. But never should there be an assumption that related negative aspects of a certain choice are simply to be accepted as "given." Some have described their first experience of the perceived intimacy of worship in a space where spoken sound is amplified minimally, thoughtfully, and discretely and music is heard in the midst of a naturally resonant space as "going to church for the first time." Careful, vigilant liturgical decision-making will encourage a beautiful, splendid, and prayerful environment for community worship.

Electronic amplification also has implications for the critically important element of encouraging participation of the congregation. If only those voices with access to microphones can be heard, whose participation is understood to be valued most? All voices must be audible. We cannot know and love one another unless we are able to communicate authentically.

Acoustical design is invisible on blueprints and colorful renderings of architectural plans, but attention to it is critical. Few other factors can have more significant consequences for the increased vitality of a congregation's liturgical participation than their ability to experience the inspiration of joining with others who share their faith.

Music Needs Appropriate Space

CONGREGATIONAL SONG

People make music anywhere, any time. Often we hum quietly for our own comfort. But music made in the midst of the congregation is not a private matter. It has implications for everyone present. The choice of music sung together in church has to do with who we are and why we have gathered. The ones who have chosen the music, and who may be leading us in singing or presenting it to us, have taken into account how that music may effect us. Music can make us feel closer to God and to one another; it can rouse our memories and rekindle our affections. The potential of music to build up the church invites and requires architectural enhancement of that potential.

Although "theater" seating (all facing forward), as found in so many of our church buildings, often disguises the concept, congregational singing is an interactive process. We are encouraged in our own singing by the sound of the voices of our sisters and brothers singing with us. Carpeted floors and/or walls or ceilings covered with acoustically absorbent tiles take away the very joy-giving sounds needed to urge us into our most enthusiastic singing. Few instruments are better able to encourage human beings to give themselves to vocal expression than another human voice. How many have been heard to remark, "I sing best when I am standing next to a strong singer?"

Hearing the voices of others who are singing reminds us of our oneness in Christ. We are both symbolically and physically one when the sounds of our individual singing voices whirl and dance together to create an entirely new aggregate. In what other way can the rhythmic activity (sounds of singing) of an entire group of people actually inhabit the same space at the same time?

ENCOURAGING MUSIC LEADERSHIP

The Book of Common Prayer (BCP) has almost no instruction about the role of the one(s) leading the congregation's sung praise and prayer. The canons of the Episcopal Church only describe the consultative role of "persons skilled in music."[18] Similar words are shown on the back of the title page of every Singer's Edition of *The Hymnal 1982* (New York: The Church Hymnal Corporation, 1985). The Psalter section (BCP, 585–808) includes words that recognize the role of musicians in the ritual life of the Hebrew people,[19] but there are only two references to musicians in the rites or rubrics of this book.[20]

However, the need for a gifted, capable and experienced musical leader of those gathered is implied by rubrics present throughout the book. At the beginning of the Holy Eucharist: Rite Two, we read, "A hymn, psalm, or anthem may be sung." This is unlikely to take place unless someone suggests a particular hymn, psalm or anthem, and further, in some way encourages the people's participation in singing it. Such music leaders may guide the singing by providing instrumental or vocal leadership. They may be lay or ordained, volunteer or salaried, and of any age. Their critical contribution to the worship life of the congregation lies in the integrity of their music making and their genuine eagerness to draw all people into worship through the power of music to attract, unify and give expression to our deepest gladness in knowing God.[21]

VOCAL ENSEMBLES

An ensemble of any kind requires coordination of the group. The gathered musicians may be able to maintain tempo and negotiate subtle expression primarily through mutual eye contact or as a result of long hours of practice together. But because rehearsal time for church choirs is likely to be limited, the role of the leader is critical, both in coordinating the musical presentation and in animating and inspiring the group.

In turn, the choir has an important role in leading the congregation's singing. The practice of a group of singers studying the art and skill of music and rehearsing together to prepare to lead the congregation is recorded as early as the fourth century *(schola cantorum)*.[22] The singers, who prepared for their liturgical leadership role by rehearsing together, bring additional musical textures to the congregation's singing.

Responsorial psalms in which the choir sings the verses and the congregation responds by singing the refrain, choir descants joined with congregational mantras, and new music introduced and taught by the choir are merely the beginning of a list of liturgical enrichments in which choir and congregation sing as partners. Choirs also bring to the congregation music that, without rehearsal, the congregation could not sing. Choral presentations offered with dedication and a prayerful attitude can bring new meaning to liturgical texts and be memorable and uplifting to the listeners. A favorable acoustical environment is essential if the congregation is to benefit from the choir's offering.

People who offer their God-given gifts to enable the congregation's music making and to offer presentations of music requiring rehearsal contribute a valid music ministry to the life of the church. The current impulse to make the choir invisible (by seating the singers among the congregation and eliminating choir vesture)[23] must be weighed against the benefits gained by the ways that sitting together heightens their ability to do their appointed task. Recognizing the particular ministry of a person or group by their particular liturgical garb obviously has benefit for a variety of worship leaders, including the musicians.

The space planned for seating a vocal ensemble is critical to the effectiveness of its liturgical contribution. The choir and the organist carefully tucked into a low-ceilinged side space cannot be expected to be helpful to the congregation. Choir and organist seated in the rear gallery normally (but not always) can see the (backs of) people one floor below, but they seldom experience themselves as part of that group. In these situations, any visual cues intended to be helpful to the congregation simply cannot be seen.

One successful placement of the choral ensemble is toward the front of the congregation and to one side, in a semi-circle which both faces the center and swings around to face the people. In some cases, the raising up (one or two steps above the floor) of that choir area is recommended.

The need for flexibility in the area of the choir seating should be considered seriously in planning. A permanent "fence" setting off the choir from the rest of the congregation has significant drawbacks. The steps up (mentioned above) benefit the choir's ability to lead by being heard over longer distances; in this case their musical offerings are projected above the physical mass of the congregation.

But musical needs of vocal and instrumental ensembles change dramatically, sometimes from week to week. Space must be available in the area surrounding the choir seating for larger numbers of singers some weeks and for instrumentalists and their stands when required. None of these people or their equipment should block the congregation's view of the liturgical action. Any acoustical deficiency that regularly requires the musicians to interrupt the liturgy by leaving their appointed place of seating to reassemble in another place before singing should be avoided or remedied.

Wherever the placement of the choir's seating, there must be a way for the singers to enter that place and leave it in a graceful fashion. Dignity in the liturgical procession can be maintained from beginning to end when space between rows of choir chairs allows easy passage for the singers. Movable seating in the choir area also contributes to flexibility for varying numbers of singers and different choir needs.

PLACEMENT OF THE ORGAN

In all probability, the pipe organ in the nave is the most expensive liturgical implement a congregation will purchase. Clear thinking will encourage architectural planning that allows maximum utilization of the organ's ability to lead and inspire the people's song. The organ builder should be chosen as early as possible so that architect and builder can collaborate for the benefit of the congregation's worship.

As in every decision made about music and liturgy, the needs of both must be considered and, when they seem to conflict, carefully and intentionally worked out.

The musician leading the congregation in singing must be able to hear and preferably to see the gathered community easily. Although singing hymns requires no explicit conducting, a clear sight line is always a stronger path for hearing, and it allows for the occasional visual cue.

When planning does not understand or honor function, frustration is inevitable. In many instances, the function that was honored at the time of design many years ago, now, has changed in fundamental ways. In such cases, dysfunction (or worse) also is inevitable. Renovation or new construction that is both satisfying and successful must intentionally seek, through a process of consensus building, to identify and honor the new priorities.

In the early twentieth century, for example, the introduction of electricity into pipe organ building revolutionized both the construction of pipe organs and their role in the liturgical and secular life of this country. First and foremost, electrical cables eliminated the need for the organ keyboard (or console) to be physically connected to the mechanism controlling the speaking pipes, as had been the case since the first organs were built more than 2,100 years ago. With this remote control possibility, the organ console could be, and often was, located on the side of the room opposite the pipes. The choir could be near either one of those musical elements, or it could be in another part of the room entirely.

While designers toyed with this dizzying freedom, physical support for the goals of music making was diminishing. Organists were presented with an impossible situation (not unlike trying to communicate on an overseas telephone call) when even a relatively short distance causes a "lag" between their playing a note and anyone's actually hearing it. This is particularly difficult to coordinate when the music has a rousing tempo. Choirs of relatively inexperienced musicians particularly are perplexed by the struggle to bring unity to a musical ensemble when organ and choir are in different places in the room.

During the same era, pipe organs built in motion picture theaters often had consoles that could be lowered out of sight on a hydraulic elevator. This was an excellent solution to the need to minimize audience distractions caused by the sight of the organist accompanying and expressing the actions and emotions of the film.

Unfortunately, many churches chose to put both organ console and organist "out of sight" too. "Pits" from which the organist can see neither the choir nor the congregation nor anything happening in the nave do not adequately serve the needs of a worshiping community. Organists who are unable to see the liturgical action cannot respond appropriately to it. They cannot see when the last person has received communion and therefore do not know when to bring the music to a close. The priest's actions at the time of the fraction also are hidden from their view so they cannot know when to begin the fraction anthem. They cannot musically anticipate the end of the wedding processional music, if they cannot see the arrival of the end of the wedding party. In such a room, the organist is also unable to see the number of people present, and, therefore, cannot know whether to plan to accompany fifty or two hundred and fifty singers, or what dynamic level will encourage, but not frighten off the congregation. Organists who cannot see and hear well what is happening in the midst of the congregation do not have an all-important "sense" of what is going on.

The installation of a closed-circuit television system in an effort to coordinate far-flung members of an intended musical ensemble (organs perched on the rood and choirs downstairs in the nave, for example) is frequently chosen as an expensive, but essential solution in an existing building. New worship spaces and renovations have an opportunity to bring musicians together in one physical area of the room, so that they can see and hear one another, and the congregation with and for whom they are making music.

A critically necessary step in the beginning of architectural planning is talking with the musicians about what is needed. As always architect, priest, and musician working together with a reliable, experienced acoustical consultant will greatly increase the success of the project.

A Summary of Principles

1. Space that is well suited for worship enables two-way visual and aural communication and opportunity for physical movement of the worshipers.

2. Planning for an excellent acoustical environment begins with the earliest discussions of the building or renovation project and includes regular review of the project's acoustical goals. Contemporary expertise and technology can help today's planners avoid the acoustical disappointments our forebears did not understand how to avoid.[24]

3. The wisdom and experience of the congregation's musicians are valuable commodities in the planning process. Early consideration of the mission of the music program and its needs can avoid expensive alterations later.

4. A good leader will be a helpful presence in the work of the church building committee. It is inevitable that people on the committee will have earnest, but differing convictions about priorities. When a choice must be made between two (or more) important values (beautiful carpet and beautiful sound) a respected discussion leader is essential. Someone who is able to shepherd the group toward a decision intended to bring greatest benefit to the community will both hasten the project's progress and increase perception that safe and reasonable discussions have led to an outcome everyone can understand and accept.

We are encouraged to become one people in worship by a space that allows and encourages us to hear or see one another. Participation in liturgy requires communication with others as we pray, sing, and use our bodies to praise the One who gives us life.

Notes

1. Acknowledging with respect Marchita Mauck's fine book, *A House for the Church.* The author acknowledges, with great gratitude, the counsel given in the preparation of this essay by Michael Doran, A.I.A., a retired architect now living in Alexandria, Virginia, whose professional services in Rochester, New York, for over forty years continue to serve that community through the many houses of worship built or renovated with his vision and collaboration. The work of Wendy Wilkinson, a music assistant at the Virginia Theological Seminary, also has been helpful in this project.

2. *American Heritage Dictionary of the English Language* (fourth edition) (Boston: Houghton Mifflin Company, 2000).

3. Edward Foley, *From Age to Age: How Christians Celebrated the Eucharist* (Chicago: Liturgy Training Publications, 1991), 6.

4. "A hymn may be sung" and/or similar statements are found more than eighty times in the Book of Common Prayer 1979 (BCP).

5. "Where rubrics indicate that a part of a service is to be 'said,' it must be understood to include 'or sung' and *vice versa,*" BCP, 14.

6. In The Holy Eucharist: Rite One, BCP 328, "After each paragraph of this prayer, the People may make an appropriate response, as directed," and, in The Holy Eucharist: Rite Two, The Prayers of the People (383–393), the people are invited to respond aloud either as their specified role in the prayers (". . . let us pray to the Lord, saying, "Lord, have mercy," 383) or as they are moved to add their petitions or thanksgivings ("In the course of the silence after each bidding, the People offer their own prayers, either silently or aloud," 385).

7. Marion J. Hatchett, "Architectural Implications of the Book of Common Prayer" in *Occasional Papers of the Standing Liturgical Commission* (New York: Church Hymnal Corporation, December 1985), 57.

8. Eric Werner, *The Sacred Bridge: The Interdependence of Liturgy and Music in Synagogue and Church during the First Millennium* (New York:

Columbia University Press, 1939), 120–121.

9. *American Heritage Dictionary of the English Language* (fourth edition) (Boston: Houghton Mifflin Company, 2000).

10. Jack M. Bethards, "Don't Give Up on Acoustics," in *The American Organist,* September 1988 (vol. 22, no. 9): 75–76.

11. Ibid, 75.

12. Ewart A. Wetherill, "Acoustics for Worship" in *The American Organist* (August 1996): 61.

13. Bethards, 75.

14. Ibid.

15. Ibid.

16. Ibid.

17. Ibid.

18. Title II, Canon 5: Of the Music of the Church: "It shall be the duty of every Member of the Clergy to see that music is used as an offering for the glory of God and as a help to the people in their worship in accordance with the Book of Common Prayer and as authorized by the rubrics or by the General Convention of this Church. To this end the Member of the Clergy shall have final authority in the administration of matters pertaining to music. In fulfilling this responsibility the Member of the Clergy shall seek assistance from persons skilled in music. Together they shall see that music is appropriate to the context in which it is used." *Constitution & Canons: Together with the Rules of Order for the Government of the Protestant Episcopal Church in the United States of America Otherwise known as the Episcopal Church, Adopted in General Conventions 1789–2000* (New York: Church Publishing Inc., 2000) 59–60.

19. Psalm 68: 25 in describing a procession into the sanctuary: "The singers go before, musicians follow after, in the midst of maidens playing upon the hand-drums."

20. One reference is the prayer "For Church Musicians and Artists" ("your servants who seek through art and music to perfect the praises offered by your people on earth" BCP, 819). The other reference is in

the rubrics concerning the liturgy for the dedication and consecration of a church : "It is desirable that all members. . .have some . . . part in the celebration, as well as the architect, builders, musicians, artists, benefactors, and friends" BCP, 566.

21. Frederick Buechner has written: "The place God calls you to is the place where your deep gladness and the world's deep hunger meet."

22. *Harvard Dictionary of Music,* ed. Willi Apel (Cambridge, Massachusetts: Belknap/Harvard Press, 1969) 756.

23. Richard Giles, *Re-pitching the Tent: Re-ordering the Church Building for Worship and Mission,* revised and expanded edition (Norwich, UK: The Canterbury Press, 1999), 199; and James F. White and Susan J. White, *Church Architecture: Building and Renovating for Christian Worship* (Nashville, TN: Abingdon Press, 1988), 85.

24. See Charles N. Clutz, "Acoustics Reassessed: An Opportunity" in *The American Organist* (December 1987): 70–71, for an account of an architect's experience of this situation.

On Round Liturgical Spaces:
Not Quite a Circular Argument

William Seth Adams

I.

Once upon a time, I had the good fortune to visit the English industrial city of Liverpool, shortly after the completion, or near completion, of their Roman Catholic and Anglican cathedrals. I was in the midst of a sabbatical stay at the University of Birmingham in the Midlands, working with J. G. Davies at the Institute for the Study of Worship and Religious Architecture. My visit to Liverpool was a "fieldtrip" related to sabbatical studies.

Liverpool Cathedral (Cathedral Church of Christ), which serves the Anglican diocese of Liverpool, is a rectilinear building, very like many earlier large English and European churches. Begun in 1904, it was dedicated in October 1978. It boasts of being the largest of the English cathedrals, splendid in its brick facade and "gothic" character. In design, though not in construction, it could have been conceived in any of the preceding five to seven centuries. It looked like a cathedral, the bricks notwithstanding.

In a way, it struck me as being what might prove to be the last of the "old" English cathedrals, ones built innocent of the liturgical awakening of the twentieth century and prideful of its consistency with certain strands of "tradition." In a subsequent conversation, the former dean of the cathedral, F. W. Dillistone, reported confidently that the cathedral had adapted to the more modern liturgy quite handily—by which he meant that the high altar had been essentially abandoned in favor of a forward altar at the crossing, surrounded on three sides by chairs.[1] This accommodation had become necessary even before the cathedral was finished. During the seventy-odd years of design and construction, much has happened in the liturgical life of the church and those developments have, in some measure, bypassed this massive building.

On the day of my Liverpool visit, after a morning's tour of the Anglican cathedral, I walked from that "gothic" and "traditional" building to what the Roman Catholics had built for themselves nearby. Metropolitan Cathedral bore absolutely no resemblance to its Anglican counterpart, except perhaps in scale. The Anglican rectangle had been countered by a Roman Catholic circle.

The difference in the impact of these two buildings on me was remarkable. At the Anglican cathedral, I walked through the space with a kind of knowing familiarity. Even in my first visit, I knew that I had "been there before." Arches, pathways, elevations, order—I had seen all that elsewhere. What I did was analyze, form opinions, evaluate, take notes and slides.

When I walked into the Metropolitan Cathedral, all I could do was sit down, and that for a good long while. I was full of marvel—overwhelmed in my senses and calm in my analytical mind. It was a striking and, to that point in my life, brand new experience.

Begun in 1962 and consecrated on the Feast of Pentecost, 1967, this building differed from the Anglican cathedral in shape, in time of construction, in liturgical accommodation or expectation, and in historical antecedents. If the Anglican cathedral was expressive of "tradition" understood in a particular fashion, the Roman Catholic cathedral was expressive of something else—imagination, wonder, even adventure.

The explorations that follow in this essay are an outgrowth of the day I spent in Liverpool and in these two buildings. The matters to be discussed are frankly related to the differences in my reactions to the two buildings. As the reader will discover, my wonderment at the daring "rotundity" of the Metropolitan Cathedral was significantly tempered as I regained the use of my "analytical mind," but my initial reaction did not disappear, then or now.

What follows is a limited consideration of the circle as a template for the design of liturgical spaces. I have chosen to look at this matter from three varied and unequally developed perspectives—story, performance, and ecclesiology. Each of these seems to lead to its own conclusions. And the conclusions of each section admittedly do not always sit so well with those of the other sections—thus there will likely be more questions posed than answers given. Nonetheless, I will attempt to make something of all this at the end.

II.

In storytelling that could easily characterize geometry, the circle would have a primary and ascendant place. Rudolf Schwarz describes it forthrightly as "the great, simple, elemental form"[2] and the medieval Italian architect Leone Battista Alberti declares, "it is manifest that nature delights principally in round figures, since we find that most things which are generated, made or directed by nature are round."[3] The circle has no beginning and no end. Its "perfection" is manifest. Whether understood as simply a perimeter or a circumference, on the one hand—something linear—or, on the other, as the outer boundary of something contained within it, the circle (and its sibling the sphere) have no equal for signaling perfection, the incontestable resolution of things.

In addition, consider how frequently it is, in common parlance, that the circle serves the geography of the heart, as it does in this small sample from the novelist Rick Bragg's story about his grandfather's world.

> It was a simple ceremony at a birth, once the hard part was
> over. The baby would be handed to a relative or a respected

neighbor or friend, usually one of the eldest, to honor them. Then the relative would carry the newborn slowly, slowly around the house, talking to it, telling it good, fine, hopeful things. They would hold the baby close to their hearts, so the child could feel that beat, and when the circle was complete the old people would give it back to the mother without a word.[4]

This "sacred circle" is the place of safety for the infant, the place of counsel and advice—"good, fine, hopeful things"—that work to the well-being of the child. The circle is the genesis place for the making of the family and the circling did the necessary work to gather the child in, and to set the child on the right path, to give the child "a little something extra." The circle was necessary by its very nature.

To this literary example, we could add countless other sorts of instances where circularity and rotundity play an important and yet incidental role in our language. "Circle the wagons," "circle of friends," "sewing circle," "curling up," "gathering round"—these are but a few instances. Yet these add their own nuances to the evidence we are gathering; they signal the variety of meanings and uses to which this image is commonly put.

In a more analytical vein, the Norwegian architect, Christian Norberg-Schulz, has explored the relationship between a human being and the occupancy of physical space, particularly in its geographical expression. In this exploration, he speaks about the ordering of what he calls "existential space."[5] He goes on to say that it is possible "to describe some basic structural properties which are common to all existential spaces. These properties are related to the archetypal relations of primitive symbolism and constitute the point of departure for any further development of spatial images and concepts." These concepts Norberg-Schulz called "places, paths and domains."[6]

As I described these "motifs" in an earlier publication, *Domains* constitute the field upon which the other two reside [places and paths]. They have a unifying function in existential space for they form a relatively unstructured ground on which places and paths appear as more pronounced figures." In one sense, domains are the "remainder"; in another, they constitute what is ordinary. *Places* are "centers," the most basic element in existential space, experienced as "insides," and typically round. They are, however, not only "goals or foci" but also "points of departure from which we orient ourselves." *Paths* can be horizontal or vertical; they are relational and interconnective; they give our existential space "a more particular structure."[7]

In this typology, it is "places" that are particularly important to our current conversation since they are understood to be "round." They are points of settlement. One goes to them and departs from them, traversing on paths. Yet, between arriving and departing, one dwells.[8] One is "in place." As Schwarz uses this figure—which he most often calls a "ring"—he finds this "the warm and inward form."[9] Indeed, his consideration of the ring as an architectural form he entitles "sacred inwardness."[10]

Moving along the same line and engaging a very similar vocabulary, Rudolf Arnheim, in *The Dynamics of Architectural Form,* writes about the way that the transept, when introduced into Gothic church buildings, creating the "crossing," transformed the building "from a channel into a place because any crossing marks a place." He continues, "Mere passage gives way to stable position. A building can be said to become a "place"...when its basic patterns occupy both horizontal dimensions, not just one. The building makes its mark."[11] A bit later, Arnheim describes the ascendancy of the centralized church plans of the Renaissance saying that "these buildings eliminate the sense of the linear path and also of the crossing, and offer instead a self-contained, closed-off dwelling place."[12]

At the same time, it is important to acknowledge the "path" that runs vertically through a "place," the vertical that runs through the circle, often understood to be the *"axis mundi,"* that around which everything revolves. Norberg-Schulz describes this vertical path as not only the connection point of earth with all that is above and below, but also as the point at which all horizontal points begin and end. In this way, it is either the end or the beginning of everything.[13]

Engaging this same matter from a different perspective is Lauren Artress's book, *Walking the Sacred Path: Rediscovering the Labyrinth as a Spiritual Tool.*[14] On the cover is clearly a circle with a very distinct center. Yet the book is about a path, the walking of which is the "centering" aspect. Arrival in any physical sense is the servant of the spiritual pilgrimage. Here we find circle, center, and path richly intermingled as images.

To this point, we are beginning to accumulate a certain set of words used to describe the nature of circular configuration—"perfect," "complete," "inward," "stable," "ingathering," "self-contained," "center," "closed-off." We add to this list from Gaston Bachelard, whose book, *The Poetics of Space,* a lyrical and imaginative excursion into more dense philosophical terrain, concludes with a consideration of "The Phenomenology of Roundness."[15]

Using what he calls "an image that is outside all realistic meaning," Bachelard describes the use of bird and birdsong by Michelet and Rilke as expressive of the nature of "solid roundness."[16] Interpreting one of Rilke's poems, Bachelard says, "The round cry of round being makes the sky round like a cupola. And in this rounded landscape, everything seems to be in repose. The round being propagates its roundness, together with the calm of all roundness." He goes on "for the dreamer of words, what calm there is in the word round. How peacefully [*sic*] it makes one's mouth. Lips and the being of breath become round." The poet "knows that when a thing becomes isolated, it becomes round, assumes a figure of being that is concentrated upon itself."[17]

To our vocabulary, Bachelard adds "repose," "calm," "isolated" and "concentrated upon itself."

We will let Carl Jung have the final word in this aspect of our considerations. In his *Man and his Symbols,* Jung offers the following summary statement:

Whether the symbol of the circle appears in primitive sun worship or modern religion, in myths or dreams, in the mandala drawn by Tibetan monks, in the ground plans of cities, or in the spherical concepts of early astronomers, it always points to the single most vital aspect of life—its ultimate wholeness.[18]

As to the use of the circle as a form for liturgical space, what have we to say at this point? On the one hand, we have the virtues our authors have recounted or intimated. Schwarz can illustrate them:

> In the ring...people were united into the warm and inward form. Their union was based on a common center....Thus each person was a little piece of the common ring. Even his own two eyes held intercourse with one another since both were directed to the near center so that together they saw one single image. Neighbor and neighbor were turned a little toward each other as they stood, for between them ran a short stretch of the ring, and the curvature which resulted when they both looked to the common heart turned them just enough toward each other so that they became one....It is this center, lying outside of each individual, which turns the neighbor into a brother and the folk into a community.[19]

Taking this a step further, when Schwarz moves from the ring to the sphere, he becomes even more expansive. "The sphere is the form of inwardly sheltered riches and of the gathered whole. Of all the figures, it is the most invulnerable..."[20]

On this reading, the circle (ring) has much to commend it, either in the practice and safety of community making or in the fueling of the romantic imagination. Face to face (obliquely), common center, inclusive, whole—these are words we would use. On the other side of the matter, the peril of exclusivity implicit in inclusivity is obvious, but more important to my mind are the implications of the circle's wholeness and perfection and the presumed safety that such a figure offers. Ought the church to gather in a configuration that suggests that we have arrived, that where we are is "perfect" or "complete"? I would argue that such a figure misrepresents our circumstances, even at the level of foretaste or anticipation. Perfection and completion are properties peculiar to God, not to ourselves or our institutions.

Further, if the liturgical space becomes a place "to curl up," a place that is persistently "calm," in "repose," "stable," "inward"—I would argue that we risk teaching ourselves falsely about the urgency and complexity of the practice of the faith. And this, surely, is perilous business, even if accomplished in the most subtle and continuous of means.

III.

Our deliberations to this point have considered the circle (or ring) primarily as a circumference or perimeter with only slight attention to what might occupy or occur in the center. We move to that matter now.

The circle that preoccupies us is the circle that contains or circumscribes the church's celebration of its sacramental life. And as with any circle, save perhaps the bagel or doughnut, what is in the middle is of considerable importance—and even in such instances as the key ring or a cross section of pipe, the presumed "emptiness" is a fundamental necessity.

If we look at gatherings that are conventionally held in circular places, bull fights and sports events come to mind. (The amphitheater will not suit here since, in fact, it is oval, not round.) In these instances, the population gathered is understood principally as an audience or as spectators, without any conscious intention to form itself into something else—its allegiance to one "side" of the contest notwithstanding. Also, as an audience, the people gathered would not consider themselves participants in the same way as those in the center. Nor would they understand themselves to be "a community"— even granting that there are times and circumstances when events on the field of play might generate something that might be construed—in a fleeting sort of way—as a form of "community." Clearly, the "fleeting" nature of this moment would limit its applicability in the current conversation.

Finally, these circular containments, the general mobility of the activity the spectators have come to watch, allow everyone to see, even if what they see at any one time is not the same, person to person. What they observe is the constellation of activities. The focus is either on the entire field or "centered" on a moving person or action.

If we turn our attention to the eucharistic gathering and think in these same categories, we come to different conclusions. The people who gather for prayer properly understand themselves to be participants, not spectators or an audience. They would understand their gathering as an expression of an extant community that is reinforced and edified every time they come together, not something "fleeting" or transitory. None of these points works against the gathering being in a circle. What challenges this, however, is the last point made above—the question of what goes on "in the middle."

Unlike sports events—or even theater in the round for that matter—the liturgy has a fixity to it, at least in certain aspects. There is obviously movement in the liturgy, sometimes a considerable abundance. What is at issue here is not a matter of immobility but rather something we might call "orientation."

A hint of what we are after here is contained in an observation one critic made about circular liturgical spaces. W. Jardine Grisbrooke, in his engagingly titled essay, "The Shape of the Liturgical Assembly: Some Third Thoughts," says that a round liturgical configuration is "completely logical architecturally and can be extremely effective aesthetically: a church, however, is meant primarily to be used, not to be looked at."[21] In Grisbrooke's view, the *utility* of a circular liturgical space—with the altar platform in the center—would depend on the segment of the circle "behind" the altar/table and ambo being occupied by "ministers, servers and singers."[22] In a fashion, and to put it

115

rather starkly, what the author is saying here is that the ministries and "presence" of these ministers is understood to be "absorbed" or "contained" in the ministry or function of the presider, thus rendering this area "behind" the altar/table and ambo "vacant."

The church's eucharistic liturgy stands in a ritual complex that constitutes the church. The actions of the liturgy are expressive of our aspirations and self-understanding, and our ritual activity impresses those aspirations and that self-understanding upon us. As Tom Driver says, these rituals are "performative actions" that carry the power to transform. In a memorable observation, Driver writes, "[transformative rituals] are more like washing machines than books. A book may be *about* washing, but the machine takes in dirty clothes and, if all goes well, transforms them into cleaner ones."[23] Moving from laundry to liturgy, what helps things "go well"? To answer that question, we take something else from Driver.

"Performative actions" are performed. This seems simple enough. And as Driver teaches us, performance occurs when "doing is combined with showing."[24] That is to say, the simple doing of the rite is not sufficient for it to be efficacious. Without the seeing, it is incomplete, perhaps even empty. This means that the "correct," "right," "faithful," "truthful," "authentic" *performance* of such a ritual involves equal portions of equally "correct," "right," "faithful," "truthful," "authentic" doing *and* seeing.

If this is so, we need to combine this fact with the matter we earlier called "orientation" in the liturgy. If the liturgy is celebrated in a circle, fully enclosed, there will be no part of the space that is "vacant." That means that some of those gathered will be "behind" the action. Given that the liturgy has an "orientation" that eventually inhibits full, fluid and rotational movement, what then? What happens if we cannot see what's being done? Does this not disenfranchise us from the "performance"? If we are disenfranchised, how can we bring "seeing" to the "doing" such that the performance "goes well"...and the clothes get clean?

Up to now, we have made no particular association between liturgy "in the round" and theater "in the round," though the associations are there to be made. It is at this point, however, that any associations would have to be put away. Granted that stage furniture is part of the theatrical setting into which the actors put themselves, the role played in liturgy by liturgical "furniture" is rather different, and the difference has its own demands.

This distinction and the matter of disenfranchisement push us into a perilous territory—one, however, that we need to enter, anticipating the particular preoccupation of the next section of this essay. The area is that of the presider and the attendant responsibilities.

The liturgy is built around certain symbolic centers, objects that invite and accompany actions at the heart of the liturgical practice of Christianity. Altar/table, ambo, font—these foci, along with the ordering of the assembly, determine the configuration of the space. It is with, upon or around these foci that the community offers its prayers. These "things" and the actions they facilitate have "standing" in the community and that "standing" makes certain demands, creating a sense of "direction," here called "orientation."

As conventionally enacted, the celebration of the liturgy expects placement, the "instantiation" of those who say/sing, touch and enact whatever the presider is charged to say/sing, touch or enact. Hearing what is sung or said, and seeing what is touched or enacted are necessary parts of the rite, instrumental to its "performance." Further, hearing and seeing the ones who say/sing, touch or enact are parts of the performance necessity as well.[25]

Further yet, and to the extent that the liturgy is dialogical, those who are to be heard and seen need also to be able to hear and see. If there are congregants behind the presider, for example, they are in some sense disenfranchised by their placement—and so is the presider. This dislocation breaks their true dialogic connection. In some sense, presider and the dislocated are not really there "together."[26] Without wanting to put it wrongly, it still seems true that if one is not within the sweep of the view of the presider, preacher, cantor or reader, then

117

one is not truly "there." This ought to render the circle, fully enclosed, suspect and finally unacceptable for the liturgical assembly.

IV.

As one reads the history of early Christian church architecture, one begins to awaken to the relationship between the configuration of the liturgical space and the church's understanding or acknowledgment of liturgical authority—and this awakening leads in turn to a set of observations about ecclesiology. Here again we will engage the presenting matter in this essay—circular liturgical space.

In *The Social Origins of Christian Architecture,* L. Michael White traces the evolution of the character of Christian liturgical spaces—and the likely motivation for this evolution. For Paul and well into the second century, "The main arena of worship assembly, including both the Eucharist and other acts of instruction and exhortation, was the communal context of the dining table in the house church."[27] One imagines here a "gathered" community, "around" the central table, though the room in question was undoubtedly "square" or some such.

White cites two factors that moved the church to a different arrangement. First, the growth of the gathered community would eventually force other considerations—like the removal of walls and then perhaps other strategies. This typically meant an elongated room, perhaps with a dais at one end. Secondly, and again having to do with growth, the number of people who gathered tended to make a true meal increasingly difficult and thus moved the community to a more stylized and symbolic form of expression. White observes that these new circumstances tended to give "a more formal order to the assembly than that expected in the dinner setting."[28] One wonders the extent to which the architecture mirrored a change in the understanding of the role of clergy—or the extent to which this spatial adaptation encouraged or accomplished a change in that understanding. This latter is

118

particularly true if the dais were to be occupied by the clergy, either exclusively or particularly. In fact, this arrangement may well have spurred the emerging distinction between "clergy" and "laity."[29]

It is not difficult to see this change, first motivated by necessity, being interpreted in subsequent generations as normative. Evidence of this kind of interpretation can be found in J.G. Davies' *The Origin and Development of Early Christian Church Architecture*.[30] Alongside the rectangular buildings characteristic of the early Christian gatherings, the author treats buildings of a circular or octagonal form, a form he describes as "an imitation of subterranean tombs."[31] Extant from the beginning of Christian architecture, these buildings were used as "memorial edifices." Over time, in the East, the rectangular style and the circular or octagonal style merged, creating the centralized form. It is in his description of this process that we glimpse the assumption of the normative character of the rectangular space.

> The building erected under this influence naturally perpetuated the traditional form of a *martyrium*...with its centralized plan and its resemblance to a tomb, but as the edifice was also to be used for the regular celebration of the liturgy which *demanded* not a vertical axis but a horizontal perspective, the architects were faced with the problem of modifying the primitive form in order to combine it with the basilica; hence arose the centralized churches as distinct from the centralized martyria, from which however they had originated.[32]

Presumably the "demand" for a horizontal axis arose from what had evolved as the earlier "norm." And this "norm," we have suggested, moved the liturgy in a "clerical" direction.

A look at Peter Hammond's *Liturgy and Architecture* puts this matter into a more modern context. Published in England in 1960, *Liturgy and Architecture* brought to voice in England issues that would come to broader expression in the documents of the Second Vatican Council. It is a book that has many uses even today.

For our purposes, what I want to underscore are Hammond's assumptions about the nature of the liturgical community and its order. And I cite these as they find their roots in the evolution of buildings to which we have pointed.

Writing about the nature of the Eucharist, Hammond says, "First, the Eucharist is a *communal* action.... Secondly, within the priestly community there is a diversity of functions; every member of the body of Christ does not have the same office."[33] A circular or octagonal plan, he says, would be "unsatisfactory" because it "fails to manifest the hierarchical gradations of functions within the worshiping community.... The relationship between sanctuary and nave must express separation *and* identity."[34]

He concludes, "the ideal setting for the eucharistic assembly is a spatial arrangement which enables the whole congregation to be gathered round a free-standing altar, but which also expresses in the relationship of nave to sanctuary the hierarchical gradation of functions within the one priestly community."[35]

By this interpretation, the "unsatisfactory" character of a circular room is grounded in its failure to accommodate "hierarchy." This being the case and if our sources are correct, what sense are we to make of the church's earliest liturgical environment, one in which "circularity" if not the circle was evident? The domestic dining room was surely such a place. It is, then, precisely at this point that we move from liturgical space into ecclesiology and a new set of questions.

Did the spatial necessities of the early gathered community "create" the distinction between clergy and laity that has characterized much of the church ever since? Did the necessities of seeing and hearing— necessities addressed by a raised dais—spur on the sense of "hierarchy" that came to characterize the church, a "hierarchy" that then became *necessary* in our buildings and our ecclesiology? If these factors aided the rise of a certain self-understanding for the church, might other factors—in our time and circumstances—give rise to other self-understandings?

Do linear, multilevel liturgical spaces create and express a "linear, multilevel" ecclesiology? At least by inference, Lettie Russell and Heather Murray Elkins would say "yes." And, also by inference, they suggest an alternative.

Elkins, writing in *Worshiping Women,* declares, "The shape of table fellowship that helps us remember to give thanks is round."[36] And Russell devotes an entire book to *Church in the Round.*[37] Neither of these writers intends to give direct counsel on the shape of the liturgical assembly—a part of the intent of the current essay—but what they offer nonetheless bears directly on the matter at hand.

Both of these authors, as well as the contributors to *In Search of a Round Table: Gender, Theology & Church Leadership* use the "round table" as the overarching metaphor for a certain understanding of ecclesiology.[38] By the use of this central image, the authors intend to challenge or "blunt" the ecclesiology of the received tradition and open a discussion that might lead in a different direction.

Russell writes, "the authority of this form of leadership [i.e., in the round] comes from connection rather than from [a] position at the top....The circular pattern is recognizable as leadership in the round and evokes other leaders to share this partnering style."[39] Later she says, "Leadership in the round seeks to move away from the traditions of ordination and orders as authority of domination and to emphasize instead authority exercised in community."[40]

Earlier, we noted Hammond's insistence on a functionally hierarchical liturgical space, a space that treated separation as a necessary and appropriate ingredient. The implications of Russell's "round" ecclesiology cut at the root of this assumption.

Further on this point, Ranjini Rebera, in an essay entitled "Power in a Discipline of Equals," argues compellingly that power can be exercised in a fashion that does not show forth dominance, that difference in function does not, of necessity, invite the imposition of hierarchy.[41] What Rebera imagines is described by Russell as a "household of freedom." She writes, "[I]f there were a household of freedom, those who dwelt in it could find a way to nurture life without paying the price of being locked into roles of permanent domination and subordination."[42]

The ecclesiology that fuels the imagination of Davies and Hammond is a hierarchical ecclesiology, an ecclesiology that "demands" [Davies' word] linear, horizontal expression; an ecclesiology that must "manifest the hierarchical gradations of functions within the worshiping community."[43] This take on the nature of the church seems to give pride of place to ordination and those possessed of its graces. Russell, Elkins and Rebera clearly suggest another option. Based on their views as a foundation, we could go on to argue that it is baptism that makes the primary and more enduring claim.

What form might the ecclesiology embedded in a "household of freedom" take for spatial expression? It seems to me that the answer here lies in the direction of a circle—all other considerations notwithstanding. And if a circle, then is our concentration to move first to the perimeter, where the shape is articulated, or to the center, the pivot around which the circle is generated? These concerns press yet another question, "How does a building/liturgical space 'announce' an ecclesiology?" And "Since what a liturgical space 'says' when it is empty may not be congruent with what is 'said' in the active celebration, it is fair to ask if the 'announced' ecclesiology is the same one enacted in the liturgy—or is it some other?"

For those persuaded of anything approximating a "round ecclesiology" and required to celebrate the church's liturgy in a severe rectilinear and hierarchical liturgical space, the dream of a circular space is palpable. I have often said that I wish it were possible to speak about the ordering of the church's liturgical community without having "order" necessitate "hierarchy." Yet, sadly, even in the common dictionary we find "hierarchy" as a synonym for "order." Perhaps it is simply built into the language. But I am persuaded that it does not have to be built into our liturgical spaces.

In the first analytical section of this essay, we tended to suggest that a circular space risks being too insular, too inward looking, too settled, perhaps even too static to serve as a proper configuration for the sacramental life of a people in movement—pilgrims, sojourners. In the second section, we explored performance issues peculiar to round settings and our puzzling tended to suggest that a truly round liturgical setting risks "disenfranchising" some members of the gathering and would thus damage the faithfulness of the "performance." In the third section, our consideration of ecclesiological matters clearly leans in favor of circular configuration as the most likely to suggest the kind of inclusive and hospitable setting the liturgy requires. So, the results are mixed.

Perhaps a way of bringing some of these views into more harmony is to pose yet another question: "If the Eucharist is a foretaste of the feast to come, what would be required of the room where such a feast is to be glimpsed and sheltered?" Put differently, "What values of the Reign of God ought the liturgical space to possess and show?" A few ideas in contribution towards an "answer":

- I have thought for a long time that a circle was the only spatial configuration in which the first might be last and the last first. If this "ordering of things" is endemic to the Reign of God, then we must surely begin with a circle and then introduce moderating considerations after that beginning.
- If a circular liturgical space were to be set within a larger room and the circle itself were open to the remainder of the room—perhaps this arrangement would soften the sense of enclosure or exclusivity that the circle seems to suggest by its very nature. The openness would allow or even foster some measure of fluidity. Something like a baldachin might "cover" the circle or "hover," as it were, yet not contain it. The edge of the circle might also be soft enough to

allow for expansion as needed.

- The space might not be a circle but rather be circular. That is, the altar/table and ambo might be set more to one "side" of the circle, thus preventing the closure of the perimeter. While keeping the circle "broken" and therefore properly "imperfect," it would also put the presider more in the community of the perimeter and less in the center. It would also preclude "disenfranchising" almost anyone. Also whatever elevations were required would be modest and be intended only to accommodate necessities.

- Such an arrangement would put the *"axis mundi"* in the midst of the gathered community, blending in a powerful way the transcendent and imminent aspects of the space. By this reading, the relationship between the "center" and the altar/table and ambo would create an appropriate (and to my mind necessary) eccentricity for the whole volume. If set spinning, it would wobble!

- At the same time, if an ecclesiology were built upon and flowed out of the waters of baptism, perhaps these waters could occupy the *"axis mundi."* In this way, the baptismal pool and its waters would be embedded within the assembly, whose orientation, however, would still be toward the altar/table and ambo. By definition and location, the water would be the center. And on baptismal days, this would be all the more true. The "making of Christians" would occur at the center.

There are doubtless other matters to raise but I will settle for just one—elevations and personnel. It was our hunch earlier that something about the association of clergy with elevations (necessary ones) worked to create a certain kind of ecclesiology, one that eventuated in a normative sort of hierarchy. Any elevations put in the room under consideration must be such that they are understood to be and are treated as the common territory of all the faithful, however associated with particular functions they may be. They must not be "quarantined" and must not suggest "privilege" unless it is that of the whole people.

This last is admittedly very difficult to accomplish if certain places in the liturgical space are virtually always reserved for the use of the same people and if these places are understood to be special or "holy" to a greater degree than other parts of the space. It is this line of reasoning that likely set the clericalization of the liturgy in motion in the first place. The more connected the liturgical ministers are within the "web" of relationships that holds the liturgical community together, the more likely it is that this difficulty can be avoided.[44] (The difficulty could also be avoided if the "special" functions or responsibilities necessary to the celebration circulated within the group and were not permanently fixed to some members "by office"—surely a scandalous suggestion!)

The conclusion we have reached, if it be that, is that for liturgical space, the circle may indeed suggest and foster a kind of ecclesiology that hints more aptly of the Reign of God than others might, but that the "story" of the circle per se must also not seduce us, and its use in "performance" must not disenfranchise some and aggrandize others.

Notes

1. Private conversation with the author in the spring of 1982, Oxford, UK.

2. Rudolf Schwarz, *The Church Incarnate: The Sacred Function of Christian Architecture* trans. Cynthia Harris (Chicago: Henry Regnery, 1958 [1938]), 35.

3. Quoted in J.G. Davies, *Temples, Churches and Mosques: A Guide to the Appreciation of Religious Architecture* (New York: Pilgrim Press, 1982), 202.

4. Rick Bragg, *Ava's Man* (New York: Alfred A. Knopf, 2001), 117.

5. Here I rely on earlier work of my own. See "An Apology for Variable Liturgical Space" in *Moving the Furniture: Liturgical Theory, Practice and Environment* (New York: Church Publishing, 1999), 130 ff. citing Christian Norberg-Schulz, *Meaning in Western Architecture* (New York: Rizzoli, 1980).

6. Ibid., 131.

7. Ibid., citing Norberg-Schulz, *Meaning in Western Architecture*, 224.

8. See Christian Norberg-Schulz, *The Concept of Dwelling: On the Way to Figurative Architecture* (New York: Rizzoli, 1985).

9. Schwarz, 116.

10. Ibid., 35.

11. Rudolf Arnheim, *The Dynamics of Architectural Form* (Berkeley CA: The University of California Press, 1977), 89.

12. Ibid., 91.

13. Norberg-Schulz, *The Concept of Dwelling*, 22–23.

14. Lauren Artress, *Walking the Sacred Path: Rediscovering the Labyrinth as a Spiritual Tool* (New York: Riverhead Books, 1995).

15. Gaston Bachelard, *The Poetics of Space*, trans. Maria Jolas (Boston: Beacon Press, 1969 [1958]).

16. Ibid., 237.

17. Ibid., 238–239.

18. Carl G. Jung and M.L. von Franz, Joseph L. Henderson, Jolande Jacobi, Amiela Jaffe, *Man and his Symbols* (New York: Doubleday and Company, 1964), 240.

19. Schwarz, 116.

20. Ibid., 48.

21. W. Jardine Grisbrooke, "The Shape of the Liturgical Assembly: Some Third Thoughts," *Research Bulletin 1972* (The University of Birmingham, UK: The Institute for the Study of Worship and Religious Architecture, ed. J. G. Davies): 41.

22. Ibid.

23. Tom Driver, *The Magic of Ritual: Our Need for Liberating Rites that Transform Our Lives and Our Communities* (San Francisco: Harper, 1991), 93.

24. Ibid., 107.

25. I do not intend here to take this to an atomistic level, saying that each must see all or hear all in order for the "performance" to be accomplished. When I speak of "disenfranchisement," I mean a structural or principled disenfranchisement, not that of discrete individuals.

26. I would make this same argument for buildings in which the choir is situated behind the preacher or presider, except to the extent that the ministries and functions of choir and liturgical ministers are understood to be "absorbed" into the ministry and function of the presider—as in the case of the Grisbrooke citation earlier.

27. L. Michael White, *The Social Origins of Christian Architecture, Volume I.* Harvard Theological Studies 42 (Valley Forge PA: Trinity Press International, 1996 [Johns Hopkins University Press, 1990]), 119.

28. Ibid., 121.

29. See the work of Alexandre Faivre in *The Emergence of the Laity in the Early Church* as discussed in my *Moving the Furniture*, 41–42.

30. J.G. Davies, *The Origin and Development of Early Christian Church Architecture* (London: SCM, 1952).

31. Ibid., 74.

32. Ibid., 51–52.

33. Peter Hammond, *Liturgy and Architecture* (New York: Columbia University Press, 1961 [1960]), 40.

34. Ibid., 41.

35. Ibid., 43-44.

36. Heather Murray Elkins, *Worshiping Women: Re-Forming God's People*

for Praise (Nashville: Abingdon, 1994), 52. My use of "round table" in what follows does not intend to ignore proclamation as a fundamental dimension of eucharistic celebration, even though it is my suspicion that my sources are not as careful about this matter as I wish they were.

37. Lettie Russell, *Church in the Round: Feminist Interpretation of the Church* (Philadelphia: Westminster/John Knox, 1993).

38. Musimbi R.A. Kanyoro, ed., *In Search of a Round Table: Gender, Theology & Church Leadership* (Geneva: WCC Publications, 1997).

39. Russell, *Church in the Round*, 57.

40. Ibid., 73.

41. Ranjini Rebera, A"Power in a Discipline of Equals," *In Search of a Round Table,* 88.

42. Lettie Russell, *Household of Freedom: Authority in Feminist Theology* (Philadelphia: Westminister, 1987), 41.

43. Davies, 51; and Hammond, 41.

44. Carol Gilligan's image cited by Sue Monk Kidd, *The Dance of the Dissident Daughter: A Woman's Journey from Christian Tradition to the Sacred Feminine* (San Francisco: Harper, 1996), 62. Characteristic here is a preference for "interconnections and the centrality of relationships" rather than "autonomy, individualism and competition."

Sacred Political Space:
An Anglican Ethos
Michael Battle

In this essay, I make the case that sacred and political spaces are meant to exist simultaneously in church buildings. The ultimate goal is to help us see that church buildings, by their nature as sacred space, should signify hospitality and justice. My argument is particularly embodied in the Anglican Church of St. George's Cathedral in Cape Town, South Africa, where we can see Christians practicing sacred space in concert with political space in healthy forms. In light of the history of the Anglican Church and its complicity in colonialism, the need to understand the relationship between political and sacred space is a keen concern for the entire Anglican Communion. In other words, we Anglicans (Episcopalians included) tend to be ambivalent toward practicing sacred and political space together, and, as a consequence, our church buildings are failing to engage the message of the gospel with the world in which we live.

In 1989, this shortcoming was brought to light as the York Consultation of the Anglican Communion explored the subject of relating the political and sacred through the concept of inculturation. The context for the York Consultation was established by an essay in which Victor Atta-Bafoe from Ghana and Philip Tovey of England made distinctions among indigenization—the development of local leadership; and adaptation—the adjustment of prayer book forms to a new context, and inculturation.[1] They defined inculturation as, "the incarnation of the Christian life and message in a particular cultural context in such a way that not only do local Christians find expression for their faith through elements proper to their culture, but also that faith and worship animate, direct and unify the culture. Inculturation in this sense is the dialogue of gospel and culture."[2]

Sacred space should reflect the burgeoning needs of those people of God who gather there. It should be a place of good acoustics, where the voices of all can be heard. Unfortunately, many Anglican Church spaces have not always supported such needs. They have not always been places of dialogue, and in some cases, only a monologue of unilateral power has prevailed. However, the results of the York Consultation help us to avoid wallowing in past mistakes. It calls us from monologue to dialogue—from dead space to acoustical space. This movement toward dialogue and integrity between sacred and political space can be seen from a number of points of view: Anglican identity and the cultural matrix of the prayer book tradition, the relationship between formation and inculturation, whose cultural form of musical instruments dominate sacred space, and specific arrangements of pews or chairs as reflective of immovable or movable sacred space.

This essay reflects the struggle to relate sacred and political realities to the above understanding of inculturation (i.e., the dialogue between gospel and culture) through the synergy between sacred and political space in the Episcopal Church and the Anglican Communion. Through a threefold process, this essay begins by examining the mutual exclusion that exists between what is called sacred space and political space, and the problems therein. Making no claims as a historian, I then will look to our Christian-Gothic tradition for clues as to how sacred and political space have fit together in the past. Finally, and more particularly, the essay concludes by studying the Anglican Church of St. George's Cathedral in South Africa, and learning about the synergy between sacred and political space there, and how it appropriately signifies hospitality and justice.

Sacred and Political: A Problem of Mutual Exclusion

For at least a century, Christians around the world have constructed a cosmology or worldview in which one "goes to church," implying the concept of church as a visceral space to enter and depart. The question "Are you going to church?" suggests that one has accepted the reality we have left the church. Of course, we understand a more accurate phrasing of the question to be, "Are you going to a sacred space in which to worship God?" However, it serves to illustrate that in many cases, we are in a difficult position, unable to live into what it means to be the *ecclesia* or the people of God apart from the identity of the building. In other words, the crucial problem is maintaining our integrity as a gathering of God's people outside a particular place. A chief concern for the Episcopal Church is to reconsider the concept of "church" as being more inclusive of both "the people of God" and as "sacred space."

In the early 1990s, I had the opportunity to live with Archbishop Desmond Tutu at Bishopscourt in Cape Town, South Africa. During that time, I learned that sacred space and church identity need not be mutually exclusive.[3] St. George's Cathedral, Cape Town, is the seat of the Anglican Archbishop and Metropolitan of the Province of Southern Africa, and during my time there, I could not recall ever seeing so many events take place in one cathedral. Political marches were led from this cathedral. Political funerals were held there. News reporters and photographers, in their roped-off section of the nave, "set up shop" as if it were their own liturgical space. Concerts and artistic events, such as quilt making to raise money for AIDS victims, continue to be staged in this place of worship. The Anglican Cathedral is sacred space because it incorporates ordinary time and space with social change.

On August 26, 2001, St. George's Cathedral became known as the People's Cathedral.[4] On that day, the cathedral was the venue for a service, with the former Archbishops of Cape Town, Desmond Tutu and Philip Russell presiding, that memorialized the struggle for South

Africa's liberation. At the heart of the service was a moving ceremony of remembrance, recalling the many communities that suffered throughout the nation's history, with a special focus on those who died during the liberation struggle. The service culminated with the dramatic unveiling of two "Liberation" panels of stained glass that completed the cathedral's stunning Great West Window. The stained glass panels celebrate the present cathedral's centennial[5] and its predecessor's sesquicentennial,[6] and symbolically depict the transformation of South African society. The event was one of the first major, public memorials celebrating this development in the life of the nation. The prayer book liturgy contained music from praise singers and drummers, choirs from the cathedral and the University of Cape Town, as well as the Cape Philharmonic. It was conducted with lavish lighting and video presentations. In the end, the media described the event as a captivating "rainbow" celebration of the new South Africa.

One can argue that St. George's Cathedral is an exception to the rule of sacred space being mutually exclusive of ordinary, political space. To be sure, such an argument was made in South Africa that religion and politics should not be mixed.[7] However, by looking to the history of the church, one can find that this debate over sacred and political space has existed for centuries. A brief account of the Gothic period will help make a case that sacred space always intends the incorporation of political space.

Political Gothic

During the month of August 2001, I had the opportunity to teach a course in "Anglican Spirituality and Inculturation,"[8] which proved to be special in several ways. First, the students were a rich consistency of thirty seminarians and newly ordained clergy from seventeen countries in the Anglican Communion. Second, the course was held at Canterbury Cathedral, England—the mother church of the Anglican Communion. Finally, and this may seem hard to believe, one of the women students, the Rev. Anita Braden from the Episcopal Diocese of Milwaukee, became the first woman to celebrate the Holy Eucharist at Canterbury Cathedral.

By this single act of celebrating the Eucharist, the Rev. Anita Braden, who, in addition to being a woman is an African-American, not only participated in creating sacred space within this most ancient place, but also simultaneously created political space. This place of worship became a crucible demonstrating the power of the gospel to change the world around us. Such events may seem out of the ordinary, but the symmetry between sacred and political space has existed in the church since the time of its early buildings.

During this time at Canterbury, not only did I learn about the symmetry between sacred and political space, but I also learned a great deal about such concerns as they are expressed through Gothic building design. The Very Rev. Robert Willis, Dean of Canterbury Cathedral, Canon Roger Symon, and John Burton, Surveyor to the Fabric, each spent considerable time in conversation with me over the architectural significance of the cathedral. A favorite quote of Dean Willis epitomizes their concern: "Architecture, of all the arts, is the one which acts the most slowly, but the most surely on the soul."[9] From these three, I synthesized the following brief history of the theological and political significance of Gothic church buildings.[10]

Between 1140 and 1270, over eighty cathedrals were built in France. They varied considerably in plan form, external appearance, size, and detail, but all had two common features—the pointed arch and ribbed vault. These two features, along with the flying buttress, commonly are seen as defining characteristics of Gothic design. However, Gothic design should not be thought of as consisting solely of novel structural features. Describing Gothic architecture solely in terms of its arches, vaults, or contents has always proved inadequate "and it remains the case that, in spite of all the books and research, little is known for certain about how master masons actually devised the layouts of their vast structures in the first place."[11] We must look at what the church buildings sought to represent, the feelings they hoped the buildings would evoke.

From the late eleventh and early twelfth centuries, Abbot Suger of France usually is attributed with having "invented" Gothic architecture. The design he sought for the new abbey church building at St. Denis is seen as an *"opus Modernum"*—a real work of modern architecture. He wanted the building to create a mystical experience of God for its inhabitants. Hans Sedlmayr wrote of Suger's St. Denis, "He did not create a sensation by any technical innovation but by his new vision of God's city of light, a positive assertion of the hereafter in this life."[12] In his own words, Suger writes,

> Thus when—out of my delight in the beauty of the house of God—the loveliness of the many-colored gems has called me away from external cares, and worthy meditation has induced me to reflect, transferring that which is material to that which is immaterial, on the diversity of the sacred virtues: then it seems to me that I see myself as a dwelling, as it were, in some strange region of the universe which neither exists in the slime of the earth nor entirely in the purity of Heaven; and that, by the grace of God, I can be transported from this inferior to the higher world in an analogical manner.[13]

For Suger, the Gothic church building was concretization of a heavenly image, and through its lavish and open structure this image was communicated to the gathered community. When Rene Magritte was asked what was behind his paintings, his answer was "a wall—I hope." If Suger had been asked what was behind his buildings, he may have answered that a wall was the last thing he wanted. While chanting *Lapides preciosi omnes muri tui* (all the stones of your walls are precious) as people deposited precious stones into the foundations of St. Denis, Suger longed for luminosity. He wanted the building to be a mysterious medium that substantiated the imminence of God, and to reflect a vision of the heavenly Jerusalem.

Of course, there were other reasons that supported the design of Gothic church buildings,[14] but theologically, we can challenge such an interpretation of sacred space by asking the question, "How does such a space acknowledge and respond to the needs of this world?" To find an answer, we can look to the buildings of the Cistercian religious order.

Under the leadership of Bernard of Clairvaux (1090–1153), the Cistercian view of church architecture contrasted with that of Suger. In 1124, Bernard wrote a letter to William of St. Thierry criticizing the monks of Cluny for not living in conformity with St. Benedict's Rule, and set out his objections in no uncertain terms. Bernard also wrote several letters to Suger voicing similar criticism, and often they are seen as opponents, especially when it came to architecture.

For the Cistercians, nothing about the church building was to detract from the worship of God; the setting was to be austere. "Owing to some well-publicized texts, such as St. Bernard's *Apologia,* written in the 1120s, and some equally well-known buildings, we have formed a clear picture of Cistercian architectural requirements.... Buildings should be simple, neutral and without colour.... There is only one statute concerning architecture: that of 1157, which prohibits stone bell towers."[15] Holiness was not to be found in lavish beauty, but in the functional purity of the daily rule. These "simple" buildings produced by the Cistercians still are some of the most magnificent places of worship, and have influenced many modern architects, including Le Corbusier, who thought Le Thoronet one of the most "modern" buildings.

In light of these contrasting expressions of church buildings, John Burton warns:

> Before we go any further, I feel that it is important to dismiss one persistent myth that dogs all discussions about the Gothic builders. These churches were not the product of

unknown and unassuming masons, who some how just managed, because of the "spirit of the age," to create great buildings. They were the product of the hard work, creative genius and dogged determination of known and named, skilled and trained designers, who were given, because of the non-standardization of language before the invention of printing, various titles. Some may have been trained as masons, but they achieve recognition and acceptance by the highest in society, as men of learning and good standing. The name architect was sometimes used, as Salzman notes, "An architect...is a man capable of envisaging a building, complete and in detail, before one stone is laid upon another, and is capable of conveying his vision.... No one can look at a great church...without knowing that it is the vision of one master mind embodied in stone."[16]

As an architect, Burton reminds us that the sacred space being built could not be seen as mutually exclusive of political space. Even though much of the literature tends to refer to Suger as the builder of St. Denis, his ideas had to be realized by his architect. St. Denis was a church, but also a political statement. Like most great cathedrals, early Gothic architects were striving to create a new architectural order, breaking from the massive and solid forms of the Romanesque, to give us something totally new, never before envisaged or indeed available to the builders of the classical period. And why? Burton believes, "...that we have to be honest and recognize that, though ostensibly built for 'the glory of God,' these great churches were political statements built by powerful and assertive people."

Of course, we will find little argument that throughout its history, both the sacred and political are contained in Canterbury Cathedral. As an example in the twelfth century, although William of Sens had won the commission to re-build a portion of the cathedral, the monks did not want him to destroy too much of the original church, so as to find a suitable resting place for the martyred political figure St. Thomas à Becket. Burton considers this shrine to Becket as an architectural masterpiece of the Englishman's ingenuity. William the Englishman, the successor to William of Sens, emphasized the shrine by raising the floor surface of the eastern chapel above that of the quire and presbytery. Then he built the crowing glory, the Corona, to house the "relic" of Becket, then making two devotional points to the saint. Burton concludes that both William the Englishman and William of Sens sought ways of glorifying the space, while celebrating the life of Becket, thereby finding the synergy between political and sacred space.

Burton teaches that, in Gothic history, one cannot separate political and sacred space. Gothic church buildings needed to demonstrate to the local populace, the pilgrim, and rival factions that sacred space was the highest artistic achievement and the most authoritative statement of opulent clerical power.[17] That, which we now know as the "Gothic" style, slowly developed not so much out of architectural necessity, but out of theological and political viewpoints. When Suger laid the foundations at St. Denis, he was searching for an architectural expression that satisfied his changing theological thoughts in a turbulent political setting. In other words, Suger's search for light and space was coterminous with his search for God and political stability.

Although we can find historic precedence for the coexistence of sacred and political space, what significance does that have for us today? Such a question leaves many peoples, especially those victimized in colonial histories, in a difficult position as to defining a healthy synthesis between sacred and the political space. If we cannot make connections between past efforts of integrating the political and sacred and current efforts, then we run the risk of never answering the subsequent question: Was this effort at Canterbury simply a "renaissance," which spun off at a tangent and therefore becomes irrelevant for twenty-first century sensibilities?[18] I think the answer is no, and one may see contemporary efforts within places of worship around the world that seek to make sense of political and sacred integration in the twenty-first century. As an illustration, we will return to St. George's Anglican Cathedral in Cape Town, South Africa, where such connections are being made.

Making Use of Sacred and Political Space

To find an opportunity in the twenty-first century for sacred and political space to come together, we look to the South African Anglican Church, particularly in their call to declare an HIV/AIDS state of emergency.

On World AIDS Day 2001, a service of commemoration was held at St. George's Cathedral. The context was needed to break the silence on the state of emergency in which record numbers of people are dying from HIV/AIDS. HIV/AIDS is both a spiritual and political problem in that the ambivalence around sexual morality and illegal use of drugs are wrapped up together. Of course, this is not just South Africa's dilemma, but all governments on the continent of Africa are being called on to declare an HIV/AIDS state of emergency.

This situation relates sacred space and political action by focusing on the transformation of traditions and practices, such as burials, that consume scarce resources and contribute to denial about HIV/AIDS, and further stigmatization of HIV/AIDS victims. By making HIV/AIDS a spiritual and liturgical problem, "we hope this will enable us to deal with this pandemic once and for all," said Archbishop of Cape Town Njongonkulu Ndungane.

To embody their convictions about political action toward solving the HIV/AIDS crisis, South African Anglican clergy organized the magnificent liturgy for World AIDS Day 2001, drawing together people from across the population. By the tradition it holds in the nation's consciousness, St. George's Cathedral has the gravity to pull together the sacred and political. Such a place and force is rare in our postmodern world in which cathedrals usually gravitate (if they do so at all) to either spirituality or justice. At worst, many cathedrals end up being museums in which priests serve as curators of artifacts and classical music. The future relevance and significance of St. George's Cathedral, not to mention the Anglican Church, depends on its ability to maintain such gravity between the sacred and the political on the bottom of Africa.

Conclusion

What we learn from Gothic history's insistence on magnificent church buildings being for all people, and from St. George's Cathedral's practice of such an ethos for all people, even for those once stigmatized as outcasts because of HIV/AIDS, is that sacred space will always in some sense coexist with political space. Anglicans are learning not to repeat the mistakes of colonialism in which places of worship were prescribed for a particular people only. No longer will paid pews be tolerated. No longer will there be monolithic European worship. No longer will the Anglican ethos represent elitist sensibilities. We learn instead that the most relevant churches are those who have learned to appropriate the fullness of light into their sacred spaces so that all of God's people can see God in their midst. God is present in the steel drums just as well as in the organ. God is just as present in the AIDS quilt draped in the narthex as God is present in the streaming banners hanging behind the altar. When we learn to practice the presence of God in our sacred spaces we inevitably learn that such presence leads us into political spheres and systems. Our task is not to run away once there, but encounter and engage the powers of the world with the sacred practices of Jesus (e.g., forgiveness, reconciliation, inclusion, healing, and Eucharist). As we know, such practices inevitably are political.

Perhaps, the Cistercian view of Bernard of Clairvaux is a proper conclusion. Bernard laid down very clearly how Cistercian buildings should be built. As was stated earlier, nothing was to be included in church buildings that would detracted from the worship of God. For

Bernard, to live in conformity with St. Benedict's Rule, and set out his objections in no uncertain terms required the integrity of living in ordinary spaces capable of containing the sacred. The simple building produces an ethos of sacred space that invites our ordinary lives to be transformed into the divine presence. The most magnificent places of worship are meant for ordinary people. This is our calling in sacred space, to participate as ourselves, and with all of our concerns, in the magnificent presence of God.

Notes

1. International Anglican Liturgical Consultations: a 14-year review, Lambeth Pre-Conference Document Reports, 1998.

2. Victor R. Atta-Bafoe and Philip Tovey, "What Does Inculturation Mean?" in *Liturgical Inculturation in the Anglican Communion,* ed. David R. Holeton (Nottingham, UK: Grove Books, 1990), 14. The authors attribute their definition to Pedro Arrupe through A. Shorter.

3. See my two books that reflect such experience: Michael Battle, *Reconciliation: The Ubuntu Theology of Desmond Tutu,* (Cleveland: The Pilgrim Press), 1997; and *The Wisdom of Desmond Tutu,* (Louisville: Westminster John Knox), 2000.

4. Anglican Church News Service (ACNS) 2602–SOUTHERN AFRICA–22 August 2001, "St. George's Cathedral, Capetown: The People's Cathedral."

5. The foundation stone of the present cathedral was laid on August 22, 1901.

6. The consecration of the first cathedral on the site occurred August 28, 1851.

7. For such an argument, refer to, "Introduction: Holding Back a Tide of Violence," in my book, *Reconciliation.*

8. For more information, refer to Michael Battle's article, "Spirituality and the Anglican Communion: Post Reflection on the Canterbury Seminarians Course," *Anglican World,* No. 105, (Eastertide): 2002.

9. Dean Robert Willis provided the following reference for this quote: Ernest Dimnet, "What We Live By," 1932.

10. I was indeed happy to receive a manuscript from John Burton who lectured the class on the architectural design of Canterbury Cathedral. To his manuscript, I am in great debt for the following information. JMB/Surveyor Sept. 2000.

11. Ibid.

12. Hans Sedlmayr, *Die Entstehung der Kathedrale* (Zurich, 1950), 235.

13. Quoted in "Gothic Architecture and Scholasticism" Erwin Panofsky.

14. John Burton offers additional reasons for Gothic church buildings being built: "Some answers include the development of structural and technical techniques; availability of materials (especially limestone), to provide more space for relics of saints, for intellectual reasons (development of scholasticism), for spiritual and theological purposes (first and foremost the place of the divine epiphany and of structured ritual), as expressions of civil power and prestige, economic conditions (number of skilled workers and availability of resources), urban development, to provide spaces full of light, to provide bigger spaces, numerological/metrological/geometrical development of platonic theory." JMB's Manuscript.

15. Nicola Coldstream, "The Mark of Eternity: The Cistercians as Builders" in *The Cistercian Abbeys of Britain: Far from the Concourse of Men,* ed. David Robinson (Kalamazoo, MI: Cistercian Publications, 1998), 35–36.

16. JMB's Manuscript.

17. Ibid. Burton goes on to say that involved in this demonstration was the architect's eccentricities. As long as the architect could penetrate the walls with larger openings, build wider and higher spaces, with greater elaboration and detail and with thinner construction than had been achieved before, then the architect found freedom to design. The history of ceiling collapses shows that architects were always pushing the boundaries of their technology. Because there are only a few examples of architectural drawings and notebooks surviving from

this period, it has sometimes been assumed, quite erroneously, that the cathedral builders were illiterate men, inventing the design as they went along. Nothing can be further from the truth. Some remarkable drawings have survived, and we know that the buildings were most carefully planned. The architects achieved an international status and were much sought after by patrons. Canterbury employed William of Sens. Reims was built by Jean d'Orbois, Prague by Peter Parler from the Rhineland. Not only did architects travel from one project to the next, it is known that they must have studied each other's work and indeed exchanged drawings. At Strasbourg, they had drawings of Notre-Dame de Paris.

18. Ibid.

House of Justice[1]
David Philippart

When dedicating a Roman Catholic church building, the bishop prays: "Here may the poor find justice, the victims of oppression, true freedom. From here may the whole world, clothed in the dignity of the children of God, enter with gladness your city of peace." What's involved in making sure that the church buildings we construct or renovate serve as towers of God's justice in their neighborhoods? It's a complicated issue; here we can only begin to sketch the parameters.

But first, what is justice? Libraries have been written in answer to this question. Let it suffice to say here that justice is being and acting in right relationship with God, with other people, and with all of creation. How can the building—a physical thing—be a sign of the proper relationship that those who dwell there have with God, amongst themselves, with other people and with all of creation? How can that building be an *effective* sign, continually (even if subtly) shaping an evermore just community? For this to happen, first and foremost people need to be able to get in and move around the church building, so accessibility is the first issue of justice.

Accessibility

It should be apparent by now that accessibility is more than adding a ramp and removing a few pews to make a wheelchair section. To be a tower of God's justice, the church building must be accessible to all people in terms of mobility, audibility and visibility.[2]

"Cultural" Accessibility

Christianity is for all people, and the word "catholic" literally means "universal." Take a look at your church building. Would Christians of other races, ethnicities, and heritages feel welcome there? Roman Catholic Bishop Edward Braxton of Lake Charles, Louisiana, wrote some years ago of trying to persuade a black seminarian to stay in the seminary. As they walked around the upper church of the Shrine of the Immaculate Conception in Washington, DC, the frustrated seminarian finally waved his arms in a broad sweep and exclaimed, "Look at this place! Look at the angels and the saints! They are all white and European. Do I really belong here?"

Making our churches culturally accessible is not mere hospitality. It is unhealthy for me as a white European-American male to believe that God is a white European-American male, to forget that Jesus, Mary, and the apostles were Jews of ancient Palestine, and not to acknowledge that saints come from all nations and races. That narrowness is called idolatry, and it leads to all sorts of injustice. The church building serves right relationship by depicting saints and angels of both genders and of different races and nations, not only my own.

Arrangement of the Assembly

How we "set up the seats" literally helps or hinders right relationships. If we say that we are the people of God and the body of Christ, yet sit as though we are an audience watching a stage play, we are not in right relationship with each other. If all the "holy stuff" is way up there, where only a few privileged members of this body are allowed to go; if the warm incandescent light shines up there while the rest of us swelter under high-intensity discharge light; if some sit in comfortable (and respectful) chairs while others are relegated to hard benches, right relationship is being threatened. Look at your church building and reflect on the literal relationship between the farthest seat and the altar to which the Lord Jesus invites all to draw near. Is it a right relationship?

"Green" and "Healthy" Buildings

Another issue of justice—one which we are only beginning to understand—has to do with our right relationship with the rest of creation. Did constructing or renovating this building respect or harm the earth? With their clock towers, bells, large glass windows, and innovative engineering, Gothic cathedrals were on the technological cutting edge of their day. Can the church buildings of the twenty-first century model the use of renewable energy sources, conservation methods and recycling technologies, exemplifying wise stewardship of God's creation? Can they be born of and then stand in right relationship with local geography and ecology?

Beauty and Bread, Both

Human beings need beauty as much as bread. A devastating and dehumanizing aspect of poverty is its material ugliness. To live and act in right relationship with God and with each other and with God's creation is to work together to create beautiful spaces that are truly public places in this era of gated communities, private beaches, and walled-off gardens. Beauty is the birthright of all of God's children, not just those who can buy it. So it is never a question of "Do we build a beautiful church or help the poor?" The proper question is "How can we build a truly beautiful church building for all people to enjoy and still house the homeless and feed the hungry?"

Respecting the Tradition by Developing It

To live and build in right relationship as members of the church means that we live and build in right relationship with our ancestors and our yet-to-be-born descendants, too. The wisdom of the church when it comes to the place of liturgy is embodied in the universal and local laws and principles that govern the construction and appoint-ment of the church's house, that is, in the tradition. But as Picasso wisely pointed out, tradition is begetting a child, not wearing your father's hat. Justice demands that we understand and undertake the tradition as a living thing, that we maintain and preserve and add to what we have inherited before we hand it on.

Consensus and Community, Not Majority Rule

How we build or renovate a church is just as important as what we end up with. Not more important, but equally so. It is more difficult, more time-consuming, and perhaps in some cases even more expen-sive, but can we make the effort to build or renovate by consensus, and not by simple majority rule? Consensus is not "lowest common denominator" design or "you can have your marble sanctuary if I can get my padded chairs" compromise, either. Consensus means arriving at that point where each one can say honestly that had I been doing this myself I might have done this or that differently, but overall we agree that this is the way to go, and we trust each other and trust the . Holy Spirit.

Right Relationships with Professionals, Workers, Artists, Artisans, and Volunteers

Like the first issue, accessibility, this should be a no-brainer, the church's natural way of acting. But it's not. Justice here means no free models, no free sketches, no free drawings, no stealing of a professional's

146

design to have parishioners execute it, and so on. It means paying just wages and not trying to save money by using non-union workers. It means knowing where the building materials come from and whether or not those who provided them were dealt with justly. It also means not abusing volunteers by expecting too much of them and not showing gratitude.

These, then, are some of the issues of building or renovating the church as a house, a tower, a beacon of God's justice.

Notes

1. Copyright © 2002 David Philippart. Used with permission. All rights reserved. This essay was first published in the February 2002 issue of *Environment & Art Letter.*

2. See the May 1991 issue of *E&A, Environment &Art Letter* (May 1991) for a further explanation of a comprehensive approach to accessibility.

Rending the Temple Veil: Holy Space in Holy Community

Donald Schell

Personal Stories and Stories of Our Church

It begins with community. In the 1950s most urban Californians, including many of my school friends, seemed to be from other parts of the country. However, my family's Presbyterian church didn't fit that pattern. My mother's parents had met and married in that church. My father's family joined when he was eleven. We attended church there three times a week—the Sunday morning preaching service (communion once a quarter), the Sunday evening evangelistic service, and the mid-week potluck meal and prayer meeting. I felt included in all this and certain that community mattered. That of which I was most certain was the goodness and deep faith of the circle of family and friends that rooted me in a lifelong pursuit of knowing God through faith, practice, and service in Jesus' name.

The faith began in Sunday school, where I learned to love Bible stories, even the hair-raising ones from the Old Testament. At age twelve, I was excited when time came to join the adults in church. I thought it would be wonderful. Instead, I found myself bored at forty-minute expository sermons and fifteen-minute pastoral prayers, hearing our pastor (whom I liked) drone on in a steady stream of words from the high central pulpit.

At this young age, I began to imagine the difference some other church building or liturgy could make. I wanted our worship to be better than this. Church community worked for me and created much of my desire for something more. The passion for the power of liturgy and good architecture began with an unsatisfied longing as I tried to imagine something I had not yet seen.

Throughout my adolescence, I daydreamed of a different kind of church, where my friends, my parents and grandparents, and all their friends could do more together than just sing two hymns. I pictured us all standing or sitting in parallel center-facing rows. Seeing each other's faces as we worshiped together, singing, praying, and listening could anchor us in the moment. In my imagined church, I wanted to pray with my eyes open. I wanted members of the congregation to catch something in another's face that would move us to experience God's presence together. I wanted a more human, more engaging way to hear the stories I loved.

When I was fourteen, our new youth minister took the young people away for a weekend retreat. On Saturday morning, he gathered us all in the retreat center's rustic dining hall. We found our places at round tables he had set with a single loaf of bread and a goblet of grape juice. He waited until we'd found places at the tables, and then, from the middle of the room, he read Paul's account of the Last Supper in 1 Corinthians. When he read that Jesus broke the bread, he asked one of us at each table to take up the loaf, break a piece, and pass the broken loaf to the next person. Then, as he read that Jesus blessed and shared the cup, we drank in turn from the goblet. The light in that dining room, the smell of bare wood planking, the feel and scent of the bread as I broke and passed it, its taste, the weight of the chalice, and the familiar, but somehow changed, scent of the grape have remained with me for years. Here was communion in Jesus' presence as I had never experienced it before.

Back home at church, we still passed silent trays containing tiny cubes of Wonder Bread and clattering trays of shot glasses filled with grape juice. Having now tasted a more literal sharing of communion,

I wanted it regularly and hoped to offer it to others.

That retreat created a new fascinating architectural problem for me. I knew it was not exactly a dining hall I wanted for sharing communion, but I was not sure what I did want. And how did this experience fit with the idea of people facing each other? I got as far as thinking of people sitting in rows, facing each other to hear the Bible, sing, pray, hear a different kind of sermon and then somehow gathering around tables for communion. I resolved to make such a church someday, if I couldn't find one.

I continued to imagine how we could free ourselves from the constraints of the church building I knew. I had a glimpse of how a church community could hold and shape the church building to its life, rather than living into the building's definition of the community. My urgent desire to reform the building and the liturgy would eventually make me an Episcopal priest. Years later, I see that my search for a new kind of sacred space and more shared action led me to a new theology, new spirituality, and new practice. Over these years, I have been discovering how liturgy can open people to God and create powerful ministering communities.

Today most Christian buildings shape our communities to a theology Jesus rejected. Christians who remember and want to live Jesus' teaching and practice must ask if the Middle Ages or even the Reformation or the Vatican II reforms offer us spaces for worship that are adequate to authentic community and lively sacraments. Like it or not, the church building and furniture literally will shape the community's ways of gathering and the ways people see and touch one another. Brick and mortar theology, our walls, our furniture, and our seating will define relationships, lines of communication, and all of the invisible dynamic aspects of community. Whether our church buildings appear loving, daring, inviting, or forbidding, each one holds a church community and defines how it can act and move.

Of course, the church community can use words to define its gathering, but if we defend (or accept) the constraints of church buildings for sentimental, nostalgic or political reasons, or if we take our inheritance from the nineteenth-century Gothic Revival as "tradition," we consent to profound and possibly ungodly limitations and constraints on what we do and who we will become. The building's voice and the choices its design represents will shout down any teaching that contradicts it. As Louis Weil, professor of liturgics at Church Divinity School of the Pacific, puts it, "Don't argue with the building, the building always wins." What Weil means is that the logic of the building will shout down any theology that contradicts it. The only argument we can win is to build (or remake) a building to say what we actually believe.

As for the Episcopal Church, we haven't argued with the building for quite some time. Over the last fifty years, some Episcopal churches have moved their altar tables a few feet out from the wall and then said that more serious renovation "will have to wait," thereby giving the building the last word. Some have built or renewed their spaces on a pattern of theater-in-the-round, which is a kind of remaking of the building's logic, but is far more limited than it may first appear. Very few Episcopal communities have found the courage to reshape the walls and seating to make it possible for the people to move. Our inherited buildings continue to shout a medieval theology in which the congregations are spectators to the liturgy.

Worship spaces that contradict our intentions and theology inevitably re-shape flesh and blood to their own wooden or stony truth. We are in the presence of our peril and opportunity. Anglican Christians who consistently claim to know God in the Incarnation and in history have been strangely willing to cede killing power to our gathering spaces. Brick and mortar, stone, wood, plaster, plywood, steel, and glass, all unyielding building materials, can prevent us from seeing, moving, or touching each other.

Probably anyone working on a church building committee hopes to build a church that welcomes people in. It is likely, as well, that any good church building committee hopes to help create a gathering place that will serve the congregation's actual theology and intentions well enough to offer us new life and holy power. But how? Large open doors and welcoming signs visible to passing strangers begin the work. But once inside, how do we enact God's presence? Do we open our experience to God's free movement among us? Or do we hold God at a distance? What is our particular theology and experience of community in Christ? How do community, grace, and calling shape our daily work and mission? A congregation's building project invites new imagining of how to live the gospel. We can shape an architectural intention by looking at the teaching and practice of Jesus, and by telling the creation stories of our communities.

Jesus' Story Teaches Us Our Mission; Can Jesus' Practice Shape Our Sacraments?

The Christian church began with Jesus' gathering together a core community of a dozen followers that he symbolically named, "the Twelve," the new Israel. Israel's prophets had already declared the identity and work of this new Israel. Four familiar passages sketch a sufficient reminder of their vision:

> You [God] prepare a Table before me in the presence of my enemies. (Psalm 23:5)
> On this mountain the Lord YHWH will make a feast for all nations. (Isaiah 25:6)
> What I desire is that you love justice and mercy and walk humbly with your God. (Micah 6:8)
> I will pour out my Spirit on all flesh. (Joel 2:28)

In these prophets' visions, holy community shines with the power of God when it welcomes enemies, strangers, and outsiders with God's own welcome. The prophets' envisioned community that could let go of a privileged place for the sake of compassion and sharing. Justice

153

would spring from that community in the power of love and mercy.

Jesus did more than promise the prophets' community was coming. Jesus made it happen. By his teaching, healing, feasting, and enacting God's justice, Jesus began creating this new community and invited his followers to share it. Religious authorities of his time took offense that he included strangers and unprepared sinners, not seeing that he feasted with them to inaugurate and enact God's work of welcoming all, pouring the Spirit out on all flesh.

Jesus practiced reconciliation in the name of God, so his community feasts broke divisions. In his last meal before he was seized and tried, Jesus predicted his brutal death as a condemned outcast and commanded his disciples to continue the feasts they had established, remembering his death so that his broken body and shed blood could reconcile all outsiders and outcasts. Then he completed his work by suffering and dying with the most despised on a cross outside the city walls. Most of his friends fled his death, in terror for their own lives.

But then, when the threat seemed less imminent, the grieving disciples arrived at his borrowed grave and found angels proclaiming his victory over death. Later, when the frightened disciples gathered to break bread behind locked doors, Jesus himself appeared among them to lead their celebration. In the locked room (and on the dusty road to the village of Emmaus) they heard him interpret and manifest how they would continue his work.

The places of revelation and awe in this story are as mundane, ordinary, and shamefully profane as a market place or a borrowed room in a poor house. Jesus' disciples embraced both the ordinary and the shameful. As they continued to experience Jesus' presence in their feasts, they elaborated his prophetic re-interpretation of his brutal and shameful death. They boldly claimed his shameful cross as a symbol of holiness and God's work.

After Jesus' resurrection, his followers welcomed both Gentile foreigners, and eventually even murderous enemies like Paul to feast with them. This community's holy space (like Jesus' holy space) was wherever the community gathered for the feast—in the countryside, the marketplace, or at the dining tables of Pharisees and sinners.

In Jerusalem, Jesus' disciples continued to observe temple ritual along with their public healing and preaching. But the temple was not their center. Everyday homes, where they met for the feast, created a different kind of center. Soon, they began modifying larger homes for liturgy and assembly. When they could, they began building public places of worship to better welcome strangers. As their places of worship developed, the post-resurrection community had so little impulse to isolate sacredness from ordinary life that their neighbors suspected they were atheists. Cosmopolitan religious consumers of the first-century Mediterranean world saw nothing in Christian sacred spaces to suggest the atmosphere of "temple."

Today, we must work to remember how those ancient church spaces broke free from the culturally pervasive patterns of temple, shrine, or sacred grove, because it was not long before the church returned to such patterns. Over its first millennium, due to a process of change in doctrine, discipline, and politics, the church gradually shifted its architecture back to a primordial human pattern, with the untouchable, set-apart sacredness of sacrificial religion.

By the early Middle Ages, isolated holy space defined church architecture. Older church buildings were re-made to add barriers and increase distance between clergy and people. Distance and barriers limited ordinary Christians to watching in safe awe as the clergy offered a holy spectacle for their benefit. New buildings included distance and barriers all the more explicitly.

Everything in the church building—furniture, fences, and eventually screens and walls—expressed this isolation. What began as a change in teaching and emphasis eventually changed the liturgy, and then the architecture, until this new architecture of sacral power and buffering distance locked Christian liturgy, community life, and theology into patterns that contradict Jesus' teaching and practice.

As a result, we can choose to hear Weil's warning not to argue with the building as either a counsel of despair or a call to action. Can we once again reshape our buildings to speak the gospel we preach and intend to live? This is the unfinished work of the liturgical reform begun in the last century.

In the mid-twentieth century, Christians of many different traditions tried to improve liturgical spaces without stopping to hear the full argument of the buildings they inherited. What they did not let themselves hear echoes on in their renovations and in many church buildings built since. Many "new" buildings still communicate a variant of an old pre-Christian (and less than Christian) message.

Should Our Churches Speak with the Archetypal Voice of Sacred Space?

To begin thinking clearly about how a building can serve a congregation, its liturgy and mission, we must consider the conventional messages of sacred spaces. In his book, *A Pattern Language,* Christopher Alexander, an important and highly regarded twentieth century architecture teacher, offers insightful and accurate observations of the familiar kinds of buildings in this culture and around the world.

He asks the reader to consider the meaning of a door and what happens on either side of an entrance space. What do walls keep in and what do they keep out? What is a window? Alexander invites us to look and watch to learn the answers. By considering what people actually do in the spaces they make for themselves, how they move in the spaces and use them, he listened for a pattern language that would teach us the purpose a space would declare for itself. Alexander pioneered a way of looking at buildings by seeing how people intuitively or purposefully structured spaces to support their actions in them. If we can see the meaning in the pattern, then we can use human choices and actions to design better and truer buildings.

In the chapter entitled, "Sacred Ground," Alexander follows his analysis of homes and various kinds of public buildings by making a useful attempt to describe the universal pattern of sacred space. It is important to note that every building, on the pattern of "sacred" as Alexander describes, contradicts Jesus' practice and teaching of holiness and our presence to God.

Jesus, in his parables and by his prophetic actions in the Gospels, deliberately overturned an old, pervasive pattern of holiness to offer something quite new. Alexander's observations make the theological importance of buildings that have not heeded that work quite clear. What Alexander describes is *very* pervasive. Most familiar buildings in Christian and other religious settings fit Alexander's description. His observations offer us crucial data for critiquing any new work of our own.

Alexander begins the chapter with a rhetorical question that he answers immediately:

> What is a church or temple? It is a place of worship, spirit, contemplation, of course. But above all, from a human point of view, it is a gateway. . . . A person comes into the world through the church. He leaves it through the church. And, at each of the important thresholds of his life, he once again steps through the church.[1]

Sacredness, for Alexander, focuses on human rituals marking developmental passages.

> The rites that accompany birth, puberty, marriage, and death are fundamental to human growth. Unless these rites are given the emotional weight they need, it is impossible for a man or woman to pass thoroughly from one stage of life to another.

> In all traditional societies, where these rites are treated with enormous power and respect, the rites, in one form or another, are supported by parts of the physical environment which have the character of gates. But of course, a gate, a gateway, by itself

cannot create a rite. But it is also true that the rites cannot
evolve in an environment which specifically ignores them or
makes them trivial. A hospital is no place for a baptism; a
funeral home makes it impossible to feel the meaning of a
funeral.[2]

Reading this as we remember that Jesus' prophetic meal liturgy
broke down barriers, we must wonder how the sacred buildings and
precincts Alexander asks us to consider could serve for communion.
Ignoring or trivializing gates, barriers, and boundaries are exactly
what Jesus did. St. Paul drove the point home in speaking of Jesus'
crucifixion "outside the gates," beyond the confines and definition of
the Holy City of Jerusalem. Jesus died outside the conventional
boundaries of holiness where he had already gone in his table fellowship with unprepared sinners. Therefore, Alexander's definition of
"sacred" describes aptly the conventional religious thinking that Jesus
overturned.

In all cultures it seems that whatever it is that is holy will
only be felt as holy, if it is hard to reach, if it requires layers of
access, waiting, levels of approach, a gradual unpeeling, gradual revelation, passage through a series of gates.[3]

The religious leaders of Jesus' day faulted him for allowing his disciples to feast with ritually unwashed hands, for welcoming sinners
who had not repented or done any cleansing ritual, and even for allowing people who were unclean sinners to touch him. Alexander reminds
us that the logic of those religious leaders appears almost everywhere:

There are many examples: the Inner City of Peking; the fact
that anyone who has audience with the Pope must wait in each
of seven waiting rooms; the Aztec sacrifices that took place on
stepped pyramids, each step closer to the sacrifice; the Ise

shrine, the most famous shrine in Japan, is a nest of precincts, each one inside the other.[4]

Certainly, these are images of reverence in the sense of awe, dread, and fear. From Asia, the Americas, and Europe, Alexander offers us a sacred imperial palace (home of an emperor-god), a sacralized center of church power, a sacrificial temple, and a sacred precinct one visits on a pilgrim journey. Alexander's broad sampling from cultures and moments in history could easily include Pilate's palace and the Jerusalem temple, the government and religious buildings of which Jesus knew. Jesus' teaching did not commend such places. On the contrary, Jesus' community making created openly accessible, explicitly non-sacrificial, non-hierarchical gatherings and said that in these gatherings God was wholly present to the people.

The temple Jesus knew was ordered like any Mediterranean temple. Just as Alexander describes and predicts, it was an inaccessible sacred space surrounded by protective (progressively less-charged and more accessible) courtyards. Thinking from the outside in, the Court of the Gentiles, the Court of Women, etc., each allowed access to fewer people until the innermost holy place was entered only once a year and by only one person.

In the temple, the faithful could glimpse the Holy of Holies down the long axis of gates from courtyard to courtyard. At the end of the axis, the temple's "veil" (probably a net-like curtain of rope) offered a muted glimpse of the space within. The temple's sanctuary differed from those in Egyptian temples because it was empty of any image of God. Through the cloud of incense and smoke offerings, and beyond the veil, there was no idol, only an empty space to image the imageless God of Israel. In this important respect, the Jerusalem temple did critique and go beyond the adjacent culture's theology and worship. Even so, its worship spoke the recognizable architectural language of controlled access and enforced distance.

To approach the sacred Holy of Holies, while being held back,

159

shaped an experience of awe and controlled transgression. To come close to something that should not be touched, as Alexander argues, brings worshipers within safe distance of the ultimate forbidding sacred space where they knew they do not belong. Distance and barrier create a feeling of approach to what is powerful, attractive, dangerous, and forbidden. This shapes an experience people call "holy."

In the gospel accounts, Jesus visited the temple to disrupt the sacred commerce that was required to maintain ritual purity for sacrifice. We speak of this in the orderly language of "Jesus cleansing the Temple." Yet, the language and impulse of "cleansing" with its precise, manageable distinction of "clean" and "unclean" is exactly what Jesus overturned with the money changers' tables and animal cages. After making the day's sacrifices impossible, Jesus claimed his Father's house should be "a house of prayer for all people." Words that could equally be said of the synagogue that all could attend, or of any of his gatherings of the Twelve.

Two other passages in the Gospels teach the un-making of the then-universal architecture of holiness. One is Jesus' prediction that not one stone would be left on another of the temple, and the other, the prophetic sign reported at his death of the rending of the temple veil from top to bottom.

The torn veil of the temple, like Jesus' teaching and meal practice, and the whole flow of the gospel narratives from all four evangelists, directly challenges this once-universal worship pattern. Because of Jesus' life and death, Christian holiness will mean something quite different and require a different architectural language.

Notice when Alexander claims he is observing a pattern that is genuinely invariant from culture to culture, he explicitly includes Christian churches in the pattern:

> Even in an ordinary Christian church, you pass first through
> the churchyard, then through the nave, then on special occa-
> sions, beyond the altar rail into the chancel and only the priest

himself is able to go into the tabernacle. The holy bread is sheltered by five layers of ever more difficult approach.[5]

Alexander accurately describes a thousand years or more of Christian church building and liturgy. By the early Middle Ages, the fearful power of human religious sensibilities had repaired and reinstated the temple pattern of holiness that Jesus defied.

Episcopal church buildings, with Gothic-Revival floor plans, conform perfectly to Alexander's description. Gathering to mark passages through critical points of life echoes the experience of a nominal Episcopalian invited to serve as a godparent at a baptism, a best man at a wedding, or a pallbearer at a funeral. Whether Alexander is a nominal Episcopalian or not, he sees church buildings like a sophisticated, appreciative tourist making an architectural tour of European cathedrals. Both sets of experiences (liturgical marking of life passages and aesthetic pilgrimages) are like visiting a shrine (or "sacred ground") protected by a shaman or temple priest. The places he describes do not fully welcome the shared actions of a holy community shaped by holy participants.

Jesus' practice implied an architecture of ongoing community with frequent feasts. His gospel contradicts the architectural message of our forbidding church buildings and demands that we open our spirits to the transforming power of the Spirit, to envision something far different. Believing that public Christian communities must welcome strangers and even enemies (a theological perspective), we must work for every opportunity to create truly public space for authentically Christian communities to worship. This requires creative architectural work of a very high order.

So what sort of public places should we build for Christian assembly? The first-century marketplace fostered chaotic inter-active community—a place where children would pipe and sing, prompting people to dance or weep. The resurrection meeting places were painfully ordinary. The stories of meeting Jesus in them live by words, touch, and food.

At this point, we can begin with two architectural principles that are consistent with Jesus' prophetic transformation of community:

1) What the Christian community does when it gathers creates and contains its holy space, and,

2) Architectural spaces for Christian community support welcoming and belonging, as well as the giving and receiving of grace-filled gifts.

Digging in Ancient Christian Tradition to Uncover New Possibilities

Louis Bouyer's book, *Liturgy and Architecture,* offers a radically different picture of early Christian sacred spaces that is based on Jewish synagogue patterns. Bouyer was a French, Roman Catholic priest, a former Lutheran, and a scholar of early Christian liturgy, spirituality, and church buildings.

Already we have observed that, through the Middle Ages, changes in church buildings served and created a more clericalized understanding of church community, as clergy ceased to be the people's leaders and became institutional professionals doing the church's work for a body of spectators. Bouyer chronicles the millennium that relentlessly imposed more conventionally sacral patterns on places of worship to make them into those Alexander describes.

Bouyer helps us to see that the Reformation (including the Anglican Reformation) attempted to bridge the medieval distance between people and community with text, but left the church buildings to speak their other language.

As an example, we Anglicans can observe that Christopher Wren's preaching halls, built after the Great Fire of London in the seventeenth century, show how profoundly the Reformation assented to clericalist pictures of liturgy and church buildings. Though Wren completely remade the pattern of church interiors, what he offered was a new shape for separating clergy authority. In these spaces, the ordained scholar and orator was raised high in his huge central pulpit. The Word that was intended to build a bridge had become a sign of division between the authority of the preacher/scholar and the passive congregation/audience/class. Most Protestant church buildings in America are descendants of Wren's seventeenth-century preaching classrooms.

In his book, Bouyer offers two powerful resources for consideration—first, his analysis of Syrian and Roman churches and Syrian synagogues from the fifth century and before, and second, his original suggestions for contemporary floor plans. He begins by observing the similarities between churches and synagogues in that period. (Remember that both "synagogue" and "ecclesia" are names, not for buildings, but for the kind of gatherings that happened in them. "Synagogue" literally means "coming-together," and "ecclesia" means "being-called-out.") In these earliest floor plans, it is easy to imagine how the communities came together and experienced—in their worship and their movement through the liturgy—who they are called out to serve. These are buildings defined not by a sacralized event, but by the gathering and shaping of a fluid community of people.

Reflecting on these floor plans, Bouyer asserts that "to have a satisfactory celebration of the Eucharist it is essential that the congregation be able to group in different ways and move freely from one [way] to the other."[6] "Satisfactory" and "essential" are strong words, not typical of Bouyer's voice. With them, he intends to offer us a strong challenge.

Moving the altar table out from the wall or even creating a centralized, theater-in-the-round space does not provide for the people to move. Moving the altar table was perhaps the least important change of the twentieth century, least important because it literally left the people unmoved. People participate by doing things. The most radical reform in the previous generation was sharing the peace and going forward to receive communion on a weekly basis. According to Bouyer, bringing out the altar table so the people could "see" the celebration only affirmed that old pattern rather than overturning it.

> [W]e must not confuse participating in the celebration with looking at it. The practice of looking curiously at the eucharistic elements themselves, especially at the time of the consecration, is a practice completely unknown to Christian antiquity.... The concentration on seeing what the officiants do, far from having ever accompanied a real participation of all in the liturgy, has appeared as a compensation for the lack of this participation, and is psychologically more or less exclusive of it.... Either you look at somebody doing something for you, instead of you, or you do it with him. You can't do both at the same time.[7]

Typical post-Vatican II reforms of church space ignore Bouyer's wisdom and simply shift from arranging the congregation like a conventional theater audience with a proscenium arch to either moving "the action" out on to a thrust stage (moving the altar table forward) or putting it in the center of the audience (liturgy-in-the-round). In other words, the congregation's seats are re-arranged, but they remain safely in them and to that extent, continue acting as an audience.

I recommend Bouyer's work to anyone planning a new church building or wanting to re-make an old one to better serve the liturgy of a gathered Christian community. The book is out of print, but it is well worth tracking down in a theological library or via a used book search on the Internet. My sketch of Bouyer's book will not do the work itself justice. However, I gladly offer something besides a full summary here: a synopsis of our story using his floor plans in old and new buildings, and our experience of making liturgies without audience.

Thirty Years, Three Congregations, and Five Spaces with Room to Move

1970–1976, THE EPISCOPAL CHURCH AT YALE UNIVERSITY

In 1970, Chaplain Rick Fabian began planning for the festal (saints' day) liturgies at the Episcopal Church at Yale University, by synthesizing the following two floor plans from Bouyer.

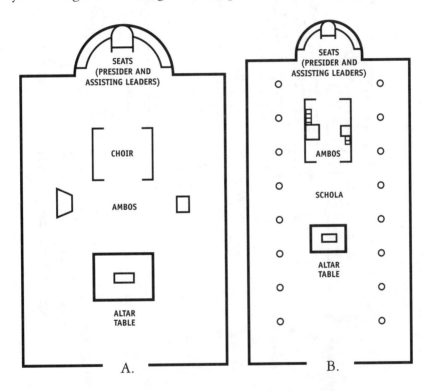

[Figure #1, Bouyer Drawings: A.) Proposed floor plan *Liturgy and Architecture* (113) B.) Early Roman adaptation of Basilica]

The existing space within which he was working was Dwight Chapel, a long, high tunnel of a Gothic Revival building with no fixed furniture. Festival liturgies in 1970 were followed, in 1971, with a daily-sung Lamplighting, Evening Office, and Eucharist that grew to an average attendance of twenty. Both the smaller and larger versions of these liturgies used this floor plan:

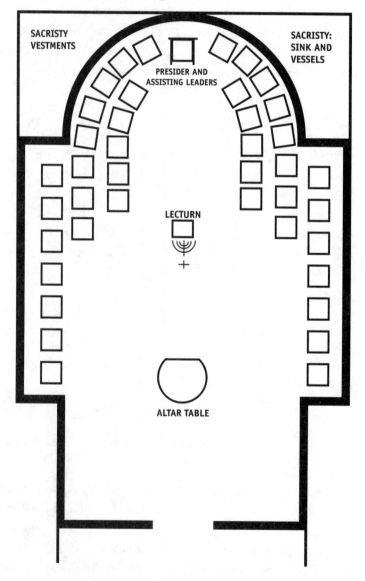

[Figure #2, Dwight Chapel Typical Floor Plan]

Notice that in turning the arrangement of Dwight Chapel completely around from its Gothic alignment, by turning away from where the old high altar would have been, to face the entrance doors, we returned the space to the ancient Roman basilica pattern.

In 1972, I joined Rick as his associate chaplain. By 1976, we used various adaptations of this arrangement for a variety of liturgies, that included both of our ordinations to the priesthood, over four years of daily Eucharists, Festival Eucharists for a variety of saints' days, an Easter Vigil with a congregation of about two hundred, baptisms (with the font in the middle of the assembly's seating), and several nuptial Eucharists, including my own.

We adhered consistently to Bouyer's principle that the liturgy and the whole assembly would move in a single direction, and the assembly together would orient itself in a single direction from the opening blessing until the dismissal.

The doors stood open until we gathered at the altar table. The open doors worked like a magnet, drawing people in to join us. Presider and deacon faced the visitors directly down the long axis. The whole congregation could see each other's faces, by virtue of the choir seating, as we offered prayers toward the altar table and later as we gathered at the altar table near the door.

From the congregation's perspective, the open doors welcomed visitors who brought a vision of the world beyond our altar table. They opened to the changing sunlight and to the daily seasonal changes on the Old Campus (a huge enclosed quadrangle with grass, mature trees, and a crisscrossing network of heavily trafficked pedestrian walks).

The congregation moving together, the ease of moving to exchange the Peace (which we offered at the altar table just before the eucharistic prayer), our sense of very immediate presence to the altar table for the eucharistic prayer, and an intimacy in administering communion were the obvious benefits of this arrangement.

A less obvious benefit was the singing. At all these services, we discovered the evangelical and community-building power of singing together, when we could see one another's faces and when the many voices converged toward us. Standing in the line of our neighbor's voice, as well as seeing and hearing one another as we sang created some marvelous experiences. The congregation found the courage to stumble through new things. By sometimes sounding very good, we were encouraged to bear with those times we did not. We began to discover that singing to the Lord a new song could be joyful.

The prayers of the people lived as I had never experienced them before. We created a litany form in which everyone could offer individual prayers out loud for the whole congregation's response. We saw and felt the grace expressed on each other's face as we prayed.

1976–1980, ST. DAVID'S EPISCOPAL CHURCH IN CALDWELL, IDAHO

When I left Yale to serve as rector of St. David's Church in Caldwell, Idaho, I continued working with this basic arrangement of worship space, though not at the main Sunday service. In a highly conflicted parish that had never seen anything but the 1928 prayer book, Sunday's work was simply to introduce the Holy Eucharist: Rite One and Rite Two of the new 1976 proposed prayer book. But with a handsome altar table built by a parishioner and a large mounted print of St. Francis' San Damiano crucifix, I created a workable chapel in an alcove of the parish hall. It had been a curtained space used for storing old chairs and other cast-off things. I began offering a new mid-week Eucharist in this simple chapel using the following floor plan:

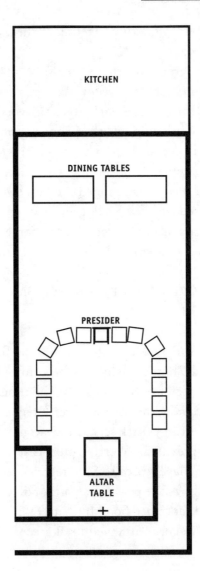

[Figure #3, St. David's Floor Plan]

A mixed core of parishioners (including both young adults and retired, older people) joyfully supported a liturgy in the chapel that included unaccompanied singing, shared silences, shared reflection on

Scripture, free prayers, gathering together at the altar table, and simple congregational dance.

I invited the congregation to begin this mid-week liturgy as a supportive community for their pastor, asking anyone who was willing to try doing some things differently to come worship in ways that I personally found nourishing. With a Sunday congregation of only around sixty-five, this mid-week liturgy steadily drew an average of twelve to fifteen people. Our sharing reflection on Scripture was lively and personal. People exchanged the Peace with untypical ease. They were surprised at how well they learned to sing together. Regular participants brought roasts and homemade pies to the weekly potluck that followed.

1978–1995, ST. GREGORY'S EPISCOPAL CHURCH, SAN FRANCISCO: TRINITY CHURCH CHAPEL

On St. Gregory's day, March 9, 1978, the first liturgy of St. Gregory's Episcopal Church was held in a borrowed chapel of Trinity Church. I was still rector of St. David's at the time. At Rick Fabian's invitation, who was now the Rector of St. Gregory's, I flew down to preside at that first liturgy. Rick served as deacon (allowing him to run the liturgy) and preached. Shortly after that beginning, Trinity Church leased that chapel space to St. Gregory's and allowed the new congregation to remove the pews, altar, altar rail, and other furniture, and to level the old sanctuary floor. In that 1892 domed Romanesque Revival space, St. Gregory's arranged itself according to the following floor plan:

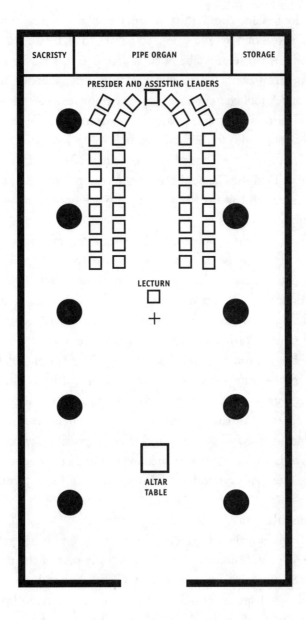

{Figure #4, St. Gregory's Floor Plan}

In the floor plan, the Trinity Chapel entrance doors appear more similar to those of Dwight Chapel at Yale than they actually were. Dwight Chapel is the only one of these five floor plans where we actually had the great doors placed just as Bouyer envisioned. The doors at Trinity Chapel looked out on a dark, windowless narthex—a problematic space for an entrance. Another concern with the entrance was voiced by people who found it difficult coming late and crossing the space to find seating without being obtrusive. We had not had that experience at Dwight Chapel because the columns offered aisles and a less obtrusive path toward the gathering space once someone stepped through the great doors.

In all these various arrangements, a single central axis oriented all our prayers from the beginning of the liturgy toward the altar table. We sat so as to see each other's faces when we prayed. Consistently, we had one distinctly ordered space and communal way of being for the ministry of the Word and prayers, and then we moved as a group into another distinctly ordered space and communal way of being for the Peace, eucharistic prayer, and communion. The simple expedient of two congregational spaces in the same liturgy literally moved the whole congregation together in a progress through the liturgy.

We are creating a liturgy of action, touch, and affect. From congregational movement and the reactions it made possible, we could reach beneath words and thoughts to the affectionate, challenging presence of people, the real ground of changes to our hearts, minds, and actions.[8]

Is this doubling of spaces economical? In Yale's Dwight Chapel, we used one common room for meetings, suppers, and other gatherings. At St. David's in Idaho, the chapel was simply part of the parish hall, and when St. Gregory's was in Trinity Chapel, everything took place in the one sacred space because we had no other. Starting from necessity, we began to discover the theological power of multi-use space, where the environment of worship defines the space. Functions that traditionally had distinct spaces, such as "parish hall" or "classroom," now take place in the worship space (rather than worship adapting itself to a part of the parish hall). Parish suppers, coffee hour, workshops, classes, parish meetings, committee meetings, an anniversary dance, our Mardi Gras talent show, and concerts all gained a depth of joy and showed their own different dimensions of holiness from taking place right in our regular worship space, often right around the altar table.

What other things have we learned from these various congregations and spaces before we built the new St. Gregory's Church in 1995? What was the shape of Christian formation and ministry in these various settings? How had our vision of community and mission grown in thirty continuous years of using such arrangements?

We conceived of the Episcopal Church at Yale as a missionary enterprise. Our work was gathering undergraduates (including several with no previous experience of Christian faith) and helping them try on a community that prayed together every day with psalmody, shared silence, prayer, and sung Eucharist. The open door and word of mouth about our liturgy drew them in. Thirty years later, those people we welcomed, baptized, and formed in that chaplaincy are shaping their own and others' community lives around just such shared prayer. Some now are clergy, church musicians, and of course, active lay leaders and teachers.

At St. David's, I created the mid-week liturgy and the parish hall chapel as my personal place of possibility. Historical circumstances (a new rector and bishop who required immediate change to the 1979 prayer book) had pushed our Sunday liturgy into painful conflict. I needed a community of prayer and a dependable setting where people could gather, experience, and share understandings. I needed a place that would invite the rest of the congregation to move past their grief and fears, and to enter into the deeper logic of prayer book change.

Some people, whose only previous experience was the 1928 prayer book, tried this alternative setting and learned the difference a more participatory, richer, shared prayer could make. They found they were learning it not just in new texts, but in shared actions, movements, and stillness.

In that conservative congregation, we struggled each Sunday to understand one another through the abrupt discovery that a decade of massive liturgical change in the Episcopal Church was completely outside that congregation's experience. The mid-week service, with its simple unaccompanied singing, silences, conversational preaching and prayer, Eucharist gathered around the altar table, and congregational dance, became an intergenerational gathering of joy, comfort, nurture, and challenge for some of the young people in the parish, as well as some of the loneliest older people. I had not anticipated such a diverse group were would be hungry for community and ready to let the liturgy touch them. Literally, it is touch and all the other non-verbal interactions that give liturgy its deepest power to change us.

In the earliest days of St. Gregory's, our gathering served primarily to build Christian community around a vision of what might be possible liturgically and organizationally. We developed a steady stream of visitors who either had left other denominations or dropped out of church for a while. By Yellow Pages advertising, our banner on the street, and word of mouth, people came to us looking for something they had felt or imagined possible in worship. Many nursed old disappointments, but also carried great hope. Many brought stories, like mine, from their youth—having found both promise and disappointment in the communities from which they came. Our weekly liturgy shaped their hope into a kind of consensus for our future and enlisted people in the work of making their dreams happen.

As we shaped this dream, we began making discoveries around creativity. From the beginning, using material we developed at Yale, St. Gregory's offered a lively musical tradition that included new texts to traditional Russian chant, plainsong, Renaissance tunes, and Early American singing traditions. We also introduced new compositions into the liturgy, which gradually invited more original work. By singing new compositions, we attracted more experienced composers and encouraged first-time ones. We asked our part-time music director to review new work and coach the composers until their new works were ready for the congregation.

We added creative programs a few at a time. They included, a monthly writers' group and annual writers' weekend, a congregational journal, a gathering of painters and visual artists, and intergenerational dramas in the liturgy. Through these programs, and adding these new ingredients a few at a time, we created a rich mix of media and a spirituality that honored original creative work as a normal part of ordinary human life. Enthusiasm for new creative work and sharp, passionate questions of faith became universal in our congregation. We did not draw people who considered themselves liturgical experts (although we were known for doing an unusually participatory, high-quality liturgy). In fact, most people said what touched them most deeply at St. Gregory's was the preaching, sermon sharing, and free prayers, followed by the singing and our welcoming them to sing.

1995–PRESENT, ST. GREGORY'S EPISCOPAL CHURCH, SAN FRANCISCO: OUR NEW CHURCH BUILDING

In 1995, a long seventeen and a half years after St. Gregory's first liturgy, we moved into the new church building we had designed with our architect, John Goldman. The following year, we won an American Institute of Architects Best Religious Building of the Year Award. The floor plan for the new church building was adapted from Bouyer's floor plan.

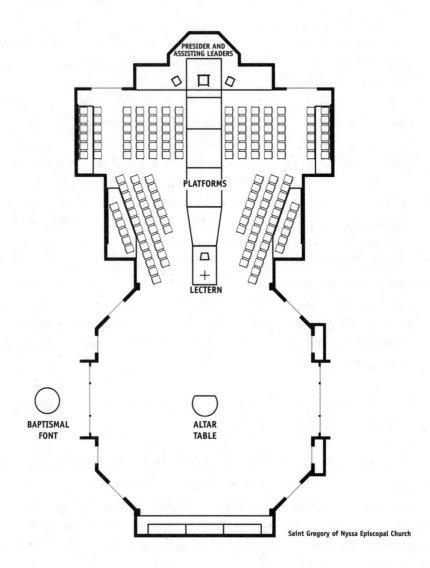

PRESIDER AND
ASSISTING LEADERS

PLATFORMS

LECTERN

BAPTISMAL
FONT

ALTAR
TABLE

Saint Gregory of Nyssa Episcopal Church

[Figure 5, St. Gregory's Episcopal Church Present Floor Plan][9]

The entrance door is located on the street side of the altar table area. The shape of our city lot requires the long axis of the building be parallel to the street. In an earlier draft of the design, the entrance was through a garden (approximately where the doors open on the baptismal font). We unconsciously imitated the garden courtyard entrance we had at Trinity Chapel, which was pretty and we were attached to it. However in doing so, we unintentionally hid the new front doors, falling into the exact kind of doors within doors, staged entrance that Alexander described in his book. We did this, even though for seventeen years people told us they had a hard time finding the entrance to Trinity Chapel. After reviewing the first draft of our plans with the Rev. Charles Fulton of the Episcopal Church Building Fund, he pointed out our hidden doors to us quite forcefully by saying, "You've done what Episcopal churches do over and over again—hiding the doors from visitors!" So we made our entrance visible from the street and asked our architect to make an obvious and powerfully inviting set of doors and porch.

After seventeen years experience of multi-use worship space at Trinity Chapel, we knew the area around the altar table would double as our parish hall. We put an adequate kitchen directly adjacent to the altar table space, so we could use the space for Eucharist at tables, in the style of Didache, or cater a wedding reception, or hold any of the other functions that tied eucharistic fellowship to other feasting tables in the church's life.

The small meditation chapel, diagonally opposite the kitchen, reflects another lesson learned from multi-use space. Since coffee hour is a continuation of our eucharistic liturgy, coffee and refreshments are brought directly to the altar table immediately following communion. Those who wanted a few moments of quiet prayer after communion requested we make a separate place. We designed the meditation chapel with no altar table. Also, it is also used for mid-week Zen/centering prayer sittings and a small weekly Taizé service of prayers around the cross. During the 10 A.M. liturgy, it becomes a Sunday school classroom.

From our experience at Trinity Chapel, we divided the sacristy into two separate areas—a vessel and food preparation area that is attached to the kitchen and a vesting area for clergy, musicians, and lay servers. This division serves us well, with the teams of people in both areas functioning differently both before and after a service.

What Did We Discover in this New Space?

We grew! After seventeen years of preparing to welcome people and having inviting doors, it paid off. The old space had become too full to allow us to grow. Now visitors came and stayed. Within the first month in our new space, the congregation doubled. In the following three years, it doubled again. We began welcoming large numbers of people with no previous church experience, and ended up performing a number of adult baptisms. New people said that the powerful building, and its welcoming doors that revealed an unobstructed, beckoning altar table within, drew them in.

Our concert and special event use soared as we cultivated relationships with musical performance groups. In the design of the building, we paid careful attention to acoustics and ways to re-arrange the space for a variety of performances. Some of our most active and generous members first walked through the doors of St. Gregory's to attend a concert. Our contracts with the musical groups require that the church's information table (listing classes, liturgies, and programs) be available during concerts.

We created a large body of new visual art for the building. This is a story in itself as we moved from being a collecting church to a creating church. Much of the work can be seen on our website. The emotionally affective power of handmade work speaks to peoples' courage to create art. But it also encourages creative, courageous action for the love of God and other people. Good Christian art moves people to see and act in new possibilities in their lives.

Our classes, including a number of courses lead by the laity, for adults and children grew even faster than our Sunday liturgy. Five to six times the number of original participants now attend.

Most recently, we see a great blossoming of energy and projects to serve the poor. How did this happen? What moves a church, that has invested energy and resources in creativity, music, art, and dance, to take on large-scale service work? Is that a drastic change of direction? For us, it is not.

A few members, who care deeply about justice and compassionate service, looked for ways to draw St. Gregory's people into this work. They moved in a way consistent with our community life and the patterns of our church building. They created a path of participation and a desire to create.

The biggest step forward came when one lay leader, seeing that St. Gregory's was enthusiastic about artistic and creative projects, heard the whimsical dream of the founders of St. Martin de Porres, our local Catholic Worker House of Hospitality. He enlisted the congregation in the making of six hundred, hand-dyed Easter eggs for Martin's meal guests on Easter day. From that beginning, a core group of volunteers began serving at Martin's each month.

On another occasion, we tried to reach out to our neighboring public middle school with an arts program for needy kids. However, the school rebuffed our initial overture, fearful that "separation of church and state" issues would make our offer illegal. Later, they came back, asking us to sponsor school uniforms for kids who could not afford them, and we easily raised enough money for the requested uniforms. When another parishioner saw the desperate need of the school's library, she asked the librarian to make a wish-list of books, thus collaborating with the librarian's imagination and creativity. For the past four years, our congregation has easily raised two to three thousand dollars a year to complete the librarian's acquisitions wish list.

Another parishioner, who is a Vietnam veteran suffering from Post-Traumatic Stress Disorder, touched people's imaginations and desires with his project for reconciliation in Laos, the country he once helped bomb. We raised money to ship a huge collection of medical supplies to that country, accompanied by our parishioner, who helped to deliver the supplies to working networks for village health care that he and a Laotian physician helped create and train.

Recently, a newly baptized member, recalling her deep feelings when first welcomed to share at the altar table, longed to share a similar blessing with the hungry poor. She experienced the grace of physical and spiritual food being freely given, and wanted to create that experience of sharing for hungry families. Feeling the immediacy of the altar table's presence among us—without rails or other barriers to keep us back, her vision was to offer hungry people their week's groceries from our altar table, recreating the eucharistic pattern of sustenance and respect. That vision grew quickly into a weekly food pantry, located in our altar table space, that provides two large bags of free groceries to the poor every Friday. It now has enrolled a hundred volunteers. Each week our congregation of neighbors and friends who need groceries is as big as our combined Sunday liturgical gatherings. Some who first came to us for groceries, are now attending liturgy and becoming members.

The new marvel of the food pantry, feeding two hundred-fifty hungry people each week with free groceries from the altar table, brings us back to Bouyer. The church building where the whole assembly can "be gathered around the altar, nothing separating from the sacred meal,"[10] in turn shapes a growing community's eucharistic ally-inspired mission. When the veil of the temple is rent, when the walls come down, truly no one remains separated from the sacred meal.

We have many, many more stories of how profoundly ordinary lives are transformed by closeness to the holy altar table, where people can approach and gather round without barriers. These are stories of people who learn each week to participate freely in liturgy with their voices, their bodies, and their movement, and learn to act in community and from community in all the ways our Eucharist tells us God acts toward humankind.

Notes

1. Christopher Alexander, Sara Ishikawa, and Murray Silverstein with Max Jacobson, Ingrid Fiksdahl King, and Shlomo Angel, *A Pattern Language: Towns, Buildings, Construction* (New York: Oxford University Press, 1977), 332.
2. Ibid.
3. Ibid., 333.
4. Ibid.
5. Ibid.
6. Louis Bouyer, *Liturgy and Architecture* (Notre Dame, IN: University of Notre Dame Press, 1967), 98.
7. Ibid., 58.
8. Refer to Thomas Lewis, Fari Amini, Richard Lannon, *A General Theory of Love* (New York: Vintage Books/Random House, 2001). The authors, who are brain researchers at the University of California at San Francisco, present recent research demonstrating that startling, difficult transformations in human behavior (repentance and inspiration to courageous, loving action) are shaped by non-verbal expressions of love in facial gestures, affect (including tone of voice), body posture, and touch. They are saying that people, who could not love, learn to love from receiving it, and those who were afraid to act, gain encouragement from others' example and support. Such observations are supported with research data. From reading their book, liturgy makes new sense as practice of divine and human love.
9. Refer to our website, www.saintgregorys.org, for diagrams and photographs of the worship space and liturgies in it.
10. Bouyer, 63.

The Making of a Cathedral
Richard Giles

My story begins one evening in early December 1998 when I returned home to my West Yorkshire vicarage (no, not the scenic bit, but the working bit—more "dark satanic mills" than "all creatures great and small") to discover a mysterious message on my voice mail. The message was from a bishop in the United States. Our tape was short, and by the time the bishop had spelt out his name, the message came to an abrupt end, leaving me with no idea from where the call came.

A perusal of the *Church of England Year Book* enabled me to track down the diocese: Pennsylvania, and the bishop: Charles E. Bennison Jr. I imagined that the call might be an enquiry about my book on liturgical space, *Re-Pitching the Tent,* or even an invitation to speak at a conference. When I finally reached Bishop Bennison, I was not prepared for the outcome. He was looking for a new dean for his cathedral in Philadelphia, and wondered whether I might be interested. He had been given my name by former Archbishop of Canterbury Robert Runcie, who, before his ordination to the episcopate, had served as principal of Cuddesdon Theological College, where I had spent two blissful years. Runcie had remained a tremendous formative influence on my life and ministry, and his subsequent passing has left us all the poorer.

I needed little prompting to consider such a move. After twelve years in Huddersfield, working as a parish priest of a multi-cultural urban parish and as bishop's officer for parish development, a period in which the design of liturgical space had become my passion, I was ready for a move and frustrated by the mysterious mills of the Church of England, which grind exceeding slowly.

Furthermore I loved America, traveling there frequently to take part in conferences on liturgical space, primarily *Form/Reform,* a gathering organized every eighteen months by the Roman Catholics. I found the States an exhilarating climate, adventurous, and progressive both theologically and liturgically, although the fact that out of one thousand participants at *Form/Reform,* Episcopalians usually numbered less than five, should have told me something.

Invited over for a snowy January weekend to be interviewed by the Cathedral Chapter, my wife, Susan, and I loved Philadelphia, and even the cathedral, filled to bursting for a diocesan consultation, didn't seem too bad at first sight. The organ thundered; the congregation sang lustily; the banners fluttered; and the ornate and polychromatic interior gave the whole event an almost Byzantine opulence.

Of course, the reality was somewhat different. On closer inspection the cathedral building, full to overflowing with obsolete furniture, was unusable as a flexible space for diocesan gatherings, and unsuitable as a place for inclusive and hospitable liturgy, overpowered as it was by the forms and images of a bygone age. Wall-to-wall pews in rigid formation confined worshipers in holding pens of passive observance of worship, while a benign and harmless Anglo-Saxon Jesus, fresh out of Sunday school, gazed impassively on the streets of a predominantly African-American neighborhood. Most depressing of all was the dark brown treacle covering every inch of timber, and there was plenty of it to be covered.

Although I have since been accused of "hating" the building, that is not so. I certainly did not fall in love with it, but nevertheless saw its potential as a liturgical gathering space of noble proportions in the basilican mode, provided that it could be simplified in style and decluttered in furnishings. A liturgical space was in there struggling to get out, but it would need an awful lot of work to rescue it.

The reality of Philadelphia, once capital of the nation and still fifth largest city in the U.S., was also an education. Those who know it are aware of its charm. Philadelphia seemed to me to have more streets of Georgian housing that any city in Britain, apart from Bath or Edinburgh, and combined all that history—Independence Hall, the Liberty Bell, et al.—with a buzzing downtown area that yet remains accessible and friendly, never overpowering. On closer examination Philadelphia is in fact the largest small town in America, a village with skyscrapers: a homey kind of place with all the advantages of an historic city and with all the disadvantages of a community set in its ways and unwilling to think big or boldly. It is also of course a city facing enormous problems, with drug-ridden areas such as parts of North Philadelphia that look like war-torn Beirut or Sarajevo.

A leading article in the *Philadelphia Inquirer* of June 18, 2000 accused the city of nurturing a "can't do" spirit, and warned all new-comers to begin learning straightaway the stock phrases necessary for survival in the City of Brotherly Love. Of these, the single most important is "Anything is impossible, if you just put your mind to it."

The writer instanced the building of Philadelphia's Museum of Art, which took a mere thirty-four years to complete, and pleaded for the city to follow the example of Baltimore, Denver, Cleveland, Seattle, and San Francisco by building the new baseball stadium downtown. Predictably, after a suitable period of going through the motions of searching for a downtown site, the mayor announced a new stadium next door to the old one, in an industrial wasteland on the edge of town. Yes, we have just seen the opening of a magnificent new sym-phony hall, but it's salutary to remember that this project, completed December 2001, was first mooted in 1908. There you go...the Philadelphia effect.

This context gives some idea of the acuteness of God's sense of humor evident in my call to Philadelphia. If the East Coast is the heartland of traditionalism, then Philadelphia is indeed its capital city. Those of us raised in other parts of the Anglican Communion are constantly astonished by the disconnect between the adventurous engagement by Episcopalians in theological and ethical questions, and the total lack of interest in questions of the form and shape of the space in which the eucharistic assembly gathers each week. The courageous, questioning, fun people of the Episcopal Church are content to inhabit museums. Clergy of outstanding gifts and tireless energy seem unaware of the impact of worship space in Christian formation, and I can see their eyes glaze over when I begin to talk about the high priority of doing something about it.

The prophetic stance of the Episcopal Church in striving to end discrimination against women and gays has led the way for many provinces of the Anglican Communion, and its authorization in 1979 of a completely *new* Book of Common Prayer (not just an *alternative* to the *real* one), put the Church of England to shame with its hedging of all possible bets in its 1980 *Alternative Service Book*.

Yet there is a sense in which the new texts of the American Church are celebrated in an old fashioned way, as if nothing really has changed, as if the Liturgical Movement never happened. All too often we appear to be a church with a "space age" ethic and a "dark age" liturgical program. It is significant that in the U.K. there exists a bi-monthly glossy magazine—*Church Building*—that features in every issue numerous projects in which existing worship spaces have been transformed in order to allow liturgy to happen. These projects are predominantly Anglican, and many of the buildings involved are medieval. Such a magazine in the United States, if it relied upon projects within the Episcopal Church, would go bankrupt after a couple of issues.

It is not that in the Episcopal Church questions of liturgical space, or of the "image" of church buildings as means of communication, are discussed and dismissed, but that they *do not even appear on the agenda*.

Take a look at the essential "package" Episcopalians expect to find when they enter a church building: a rusty St. George's shield, red doors and red carpets, gloomy interiors in which you can barely see a hand in front of you, pews and more pews, choir stalls filling the chancel, a pipe organ, fenced altars, pointed windows, and as large an acreage as possible of wood paneling, stained dark brown—all combined in a liturgical space of bowling alley proportions, utterly inappropriate for expressing the theology of participation and inclusion. These features are more than decorative detail; for many Episcopalians, they define the essential character of our ecclesiastical allegiance. The opacity of the stained glass is a litmus test of the utmost importance, a precise measure of our authenticity as religionists of the old order.

Whenever we pay little or no attention to the details of our worshiping environment (other than to keep things exactly as they have always been) we defy not only the experience of the mainstream liturgical churches in recognizing environment as a key factor in liturgical formation, but our own experience too, in every walk of life. We are all affected to an incredible degree by how the rooms and places and neighborhoods we inhabit look and feel. Statistics are available in truckloads to show how human behavior and performance are directly related to the color, light, and quality of our surroundings, whether it be the classroom or the workplace or even the prison.

In marginalizing questions of liturgical space, we also reveal ourselves as, at depth, non-sacramental, i.e., the environment of worship is no longer an outward and visible sign of an inward and invisible grace as we encounter God afresh in the language and posture of today.

The causes of this fixation with the past are various, but warrant urgent examination if the Episcopal Church is to survive. For this, we need people who know what they are talking about, rather than someone whose green card is freshly minted. Yet, perhaps I might be allowed to suggest a few clues:

1. There is an understandable desire to make the most of what history we have accrued over the last three centuries, and it is certainly good stewardship to care responsibly for the treasures of the past put into our hands. However, there are three problem areas arising from this emphasis on historic preservation:

a) A tendency to mistake recent American ecclesiastical history with our "tradition" within the Anglican Communion, reducing us to a "Protestant" denomination with little sense of our "Catholic" past stretching back two thousand years.

b) A lack of critical judgment in regard to old buildings. "If it's old it must be good" is no way to ensure that the best is recognized and treasured. The superlatives heaped by the preservationists upon our modest little cathedral in Philadelphia leave those of us who use the place both bemused and amused.

c) The lack of understanding that memorial *gifts* are gifts, not objects of leverage left by the church of the past to inhibit the church of the present, like some historical hand grenades ready to blow up when we touch them. Hopefully in our private lives, we do not continually check out what has happened to the gifts we have given friends. They were gifts, the joy was in the giving. There is no reason why gifts to churches should be viewed any differently.

2. The desire to emphasize our church's link with the "Old Country" leads us to preserve architectural features which we imagine to be the norm in the church over there. This is often based on faulty information. As pointed out above, the church in England is busy renovating worship spaces with a determination and vigor that would amaze Americans, and ironically the very features that we imagine to be English—e.g. wooden paneling around nave walls—are relatively rare in England. An American Gothic interior has its own character that really could come from nowhere else. In only exceptional cases could they be mistaken for an English interior.

3. The polity of the Episcopal Church is apparently geared to enslave the church forever in a maintenance mode. It is often alleged that it is in fact a congregational church with purple shirts, and my own experience so far does nothing to dispel that idea. Bishops have very little authority in the face of strong parishes to which they are often financially beholden. The power of the local congregation to go its own way, to defy the diocesan bishop or defect from the common life of the diocese, tends to perpetuate parochialism and work aggressively against change of any kind. In particular, the power of the local vestry to hire and fire clergy, and the vestry's role as paymaster, undermine the independent role of the pastor as the conscience of the people. The prophet has a hard time, while the ever-affirming sustainer of the status quo goes well rewarded. Here may well be the seeds of inevitable decline and eventual disintegration.

4. Congregationalism, in turn, serves to foster a lack of awareness of the critical missionary situation faced by mainstream churches in the Western world. If things look very much as they have always done, and people are still coming, albeit fewer in number and older in age, we need not worry.

5. Our seminaries (and this is true on both sides of the Atlantic) make no provision for training ordinands in the management of change. This is because, by and large, *it is not expected.* Ordination today is seen above all as a commissioning to take care of that and those entrusted to us. Those charged to "take care" very easily become those who merely "care take" (i.e., who serve as janitors for the people of God). Missionaries and prophets, and those willing to shake up the local church for the sake of the Kingdom of God, are in short supply in our

ranks. Indeed the unforgivable sin for clergy is still considered to be that of losing someone from the congregation, whereas a parting of the ways may be the first step in the renewal of congregational life.

6. Our comparative isolation from other mainstream liturgical traditions—most notably the Roman Church—means that we have not been affected as we might have been by such forces for change as the Second Vatican Council. No Roman Catholic church building in the United States has remained unaffected in its interior appearance by Vatican II, yet we have learned nothing from this. Likewise, we have not learned any new tunes to sing, using our hymnals as shields to repel all interlopers armed with the rich and varied material available from other traditions.

Given this cultural liturgical setting, the renovation of a diocesan cathedral has dynamite potential in terms of modeling a new approach which liberates our worship from the spaces in which it is constrained.

Bishop Bennison is a man of vision who longs to see his diocese transformed. On becoming diocesan bishop in 1998, he initiated a process of consultation aimed at energizing the diocese with a new vision for the future. The culmination of this process was the approval, by diocesan convention in November 2001, of the strategic plan called, Our Holy Experiment, the title of which borrows a phrase from William Penn, the Quaker founder of the Commonwealth of Pennsylvania.

Our Holy Experiment identifies the cathedral as one of four essential elements, along with congregational development, campus ministry, and a camp and conference center, that will help re-equip the diocese for the future. The cathedral is especially significant, not only because it is in itself a key component, but because it will serve to embody the other key components and the whole plan, by recalling the diocese to its new journey every time it gathers in the transformed cathedral space.

In this role the cathedral space will, by its totally changed appearance and greatly enhanced facilities, become a teaching aid and formation tool. It will spell out with force and clarity the theological rationale undergirding the diocesan strategic plan, a rationale common to many different movements and agencies that have sought to renew the Christian church over the last hundred years. Common to these movements has been a renewed emphasis on the role of the community of the baptized, rather than the hierarchy of ordained priesthood, as the body of ministry that is set apart, made holy, and empowered by God. This community is called to be a new creation of grace and love, changing the world in so far as it is changed itself. We are witnessing nothing less than a second Reformation.

Robert Warren, that gifted pastor, writer, and missioner of the English Church, reminds us that Christians today are called, no longer to "go to church," but to *be* church.[1] In that simple statement lies a rediscovery of Christianity that is light years away from the experience of church even of my boyhood. We have come of age, and must claim our birthright. Our cathedral project can therefore be seen as a kind of "theological claims office," where we assemble to ask God's mercy and grace that we may become what we are. Augustine of Hippo, troubled theologian but king of the sound bite, put it so well in words which we often use when sharing Holy Communion at the cathedral: "Receive what you are, the body of Christ."[2]

The Diocese of Pennsylvania, constituted in 1784, had made several attempts in its long history to create a cathedral—one massive scheme involved a three-hundred foot tower on a hill overlooking the city— but all came to naught until the arrival of a bishop who had been a cathedral dean himself and determined to do something about the anomaly. Former Bishop Allen Bartlett (1986–1998) set in motion a process that culminated in 1992 in the designation of the Church of the Saviour as the diocesan cathedral.

The Church of the Saviour was a neighborhood church, west of center city, that had fallen on hard times, having been a prominent church between the World Wars. It was large, enjoyed a good location between the campus of the University of Pennsylvania and the cosmopolitan neighborhood of West Philadelphia, and it had some endowment. It was billed as a project which would cost the diocese nothing; this was no doubt an unavoidable tactic at the time, but a short-sighted one.

The building itself dates from 1906, when the noted Philadelphia architect Charles W. Burns, Jr. had a second bite at the cherry of designing a church for this site on 38th Street. In 1889, he had extensively remodeled an earlier stone building erected in 1856, but following a disastrous fire he could really go to town, and produced a massive brownstone structure. The style is described as Italian Romanesque, but perhaps Mr. Burns had never been to Italy.

It is in fact a mixture of styles, with an English hammer-beam roof over-arching a debased Romanesque nave, in which the piers are out of proportion with the capitals they support. The murals by Edwin Blashfield at the east end produce a powerful tour-de-force, but they are not enhanced by the frenzied decorative busyness of the whole space, in which anything that stood still for half-an-hour was stenciled upon. The nave walls were muddy brown, the stained glass windows allowed very little natural light to penetrate, and the whole effect spread doom and gloom. A 1981 restoration had tried, at great expense, to "lift" the interior, and gave it some sparkle for a time, until the light bulbs (fixed in the roof space sixty-five feet beyond reach) gave up the ghost one by one.

Outside, the building has a squat appearance, resulting from the campanile not having been built high enough to be in scale with the rest of the building, and it fails to dominate the street scene. It is not a great building by any stretch of the imagination, but is a good one, capable of becoming even better.

Notwithstanding these defects, and no doubt largely because of the fine east-end murals, the building was placed on the National Register of Historic Places in 1979. It is praised by preservationists as "the most complete, the most perfectly preserved" Victorian church building in the city.

Certainly the building now seems able to arouse passionate opinions. One local observer went so far as to liken the treasures of the cathedral's interior to the great statues of the Buddha in Afghanistan destroyed by the Taliban, thereby putting us right up there with the Taj Mahal, while others preferred a comparison of its ostentatious interior to the vulgarity of a Turkish harem, and could not wait for someone to do something—anything—with this monstrous barn.

So what actually happened? The first dean, Jack Hardwick, a gifted pastor who had been rector of the former church, retired in 1993, and after an interim period he was succeeded in 1996 by Wayland Melton, who immediately recognized the problems posed by the rigid and inflexible seating plan. He began the process of removing the pews, clearing spaces at both the front and the rear of the nave. But his untimely death, after less than one year in office, brought such changes to an end.

Although the front choir stalls were removed by Interim Dean Jack Shepherd (1997–1999), on my arrival in July 1999 the interior of the building looked very much as it always had, with the (unused) high altar and (unused) choir stalls still in place, complete with chancel and altar railings. Moreover, the ethos of the place continued to call the shots, dragging the worshiping community back into the past. Despite the best efforts to renew liturgy and to move ahead, the building always won.

The story of the renovation can be divided up into several distinct steps over a three-year period.

1. Alterations to the Existing Space, 1999

The first step was to clear more space to allow the liturgy to breathe, and at the same time inscribe some "writing on the wall" that would make clear the direction in which things were to go from now on.

"How soon could you get the rest of the pews out?" was the question asked by members of the Cathedral Chapter at my interview in January 1999. So without further ado, the clearances began. At this point it is worth noting that the Chapter is a body consisting of fifteen members of the diocese, clergy and lay, of which three were members of the cathedral congregation, and which is chaired by the bishop. This built-in majority of the wider diocesan constituency is a major factor in enabling the cathedral to embrace change more readily than a local church.

At the same time however, so daunted was I by the task of taming this heavy and ponderous giant of a building, that I began to look around the city for other possibilities for a cathedral center. Apart from the architectural problems posed by the building, the site was severely restricted. What alternatives were there to existing ecclesiastical buildings?

Trying to think outside the box, I consulted realtors about commercial buildings standing empty, and about the site of the former Philadelphia Divinity School (sadly closed in the 1970s and sold for a song) which formed one whole block nearby, large enough to accommodate a whole diocesan center, and which still included its magnificent chapel. The site's new owners, the University of Pennsylvania, were however about to build a new neighborhood school on the site. Eventually I was forced to conclude that there was no viable alternative that I would stand a chance of "selling" to the diocesan convention, and that the existing cathedral, despite its shortcomings, remained the best bet.

So we got to work on it, and within a few months of my arrival, and with chapter approval, the chancel was cleared of furniture to create a liturgical platform for diocesan occasions. Choir stalls, chancel rails, and altar rails were all removed, and where the paneling behind the rear stalls had been, the walls were painted white. The stone high altar remained in place, but divested of all furnishings, and the large pulpit was retained on the south side of the chancel arch. In addition, more pews were removed from the west end to make room for a "liturgy of journey" at the Sunday Eucharist, in which the assembly would gather at the west end around a temporary font for the liturgy of the Word, moving at the offertory to stand around a square altar table at the head of the nave for the eucharistic prayer.

Painting the chancel walls white proved to be a most effective means of getting everyone to the edge of their seats and causing those previously uninvolved to take a view on what should be done. It was the visual equivalent of firing the ninety-nine-year-old choir director: painful but necessary.

2. Consulting and Planning, 2000

The alterations to the existing building were recognized as merely temporary, just the first provisional steps in a long process of rethinking the space theologically, and we had to begin thinking more comprehensively.

The first task was for the chapter to appoint a cathedral architect, and great care was taken over this process, drawing up a short list of six candidates who were experienced in the conservation (as opposed to preservation) of old buildings, and who had liturgical experience and sensitivity. As is usually the case in such circumstances, we liked them all and had a difficult time coming to a conclusion. Eventually we chose George Yu, born in Shanghai and trained at the University of Pennsylvania under Louis Kahn, who had wide experience of creating beautiful liturgical spaces—both new and renovated—in Roman, Lutheran, and Presbyterian traditions. He had worked on over twenty-five church related projects, and as an excellent listener and communicator, is skilled at getting alongside varied groups and enlisting their help in the design process. Yu began work on a master plan for us in March 2000, immediately initiating an extensive consultation process involving every group and parish and level of

195

authority in the diocese.

At this point Bishop Bennison asked me, "Richard, why are you in such a hurry?" To which, I replied, "I'm nearly 60 years old and these things take for ever!" Furthermore, my coming three thousand miles to do this job, at considerable inconvenience to those dearest to me, honed my natural impatience to a keen edge.

I did not have to wait long. Because we wanted to continue the clearance of pews in the nave, George thought it wise to authorize a further structural engineer's survey to make sure that the floor could take the increased loading which pew removal produces. The nave floor had cracks in the terrazzo section, and undulations visible to the naked eye, and had been causing concern for many years.

My hope was that the survey would offer no reason why the rest of the pews could not be removed forthwith, but instead to my dismay the survey told us that *nothing* could be moved. A structure which was meant to bear loads of one hundred pounds per square foot was found to be capable of supporting only thirty pounds, an unacceptable level for a place of public assembly. This came to light in July 2000, only weeks after a pier collapse at a nightclub on the River Delaware had resulted in the deaths of several young people, attracting national press attention. Our diocesan chancellor's office advised immediate closure of the building.

Despite these expert opinions, both structural and legal, such was the climate of suspicion in the diocese at that time that the closure was regarded by some as nothing more than a ruse by the wily dean.

The skepticism of those opposed to change was understandable. Suddenly, the cathedral building, previously understood to be a sound structure requiring no major expenditure, was declared unusable, and the long-term renovation proposals were suddenly hot on the plate. Or were they?

First, the chapter had to take a view as to whether vast expenditure on this building would be appropriate. Was it better to cut our losses, sell the building to the university, and look elsewhere? The timing of events was not good. The diocesan strategic plan envisaged a huge capital appeal in 2003, and a cathedral appeal before that could have thrown a wrench in the works.

Towards the end of 2000, a further complication arose when the chapter was given the option of purchasing an adjoining apartment building. This was a godsend in terms of realizing the dream of establishing a diocesan headquarters on an enlarged cathedral site, but threatened to stretch available funds to a breaking point.

Eventually, the chapter concluded that the existing cathedral site remained the best option. This was the rainy day that endowment funds were meant for, and the money should be spent. It was no good having money in the bank and no cathedral. Accordingly, George Yu was authorized to draw up a detailed design for a radically re-ordered worship space, to be funded entirely from chapter funds. At the same time the chapter resolved to pursue the property acquisition, with the help of a commercial loan or in partnership with the diocese.[3]

These decisions were taken in the knowledge that funds would not stretch to the renovation of the undercroft, but there was no alternative to this strategic risk. We took comfort from the example of Philadelphia Museum of Art, which had deliberately built the two wings first, on the reasonable assumption that the central block joining them would follow inevitably. Likewise the chapter considered that, if the worship space could be renovated with sufficient élan, then the restrooms would follow.

The closure of the cathedral building meant that big events, such as ordinations, and the diocesan convention, were dispersed to other venues around the diocese, while Sunday worship for our small but growing congregation was transferred into the cathedral house. Here we were able to continue our "liturgy of journey" by using two rooms on the ground floor, one for the liturgy of the Word, and the other for the liturgy of the breaking of bread. We also used the entrance vestibule as a baptistry for some seasons of the year, where we assembled around the font for the penitential rite and sprinkling before taking our places in the room of the Word.

Towards the end of 2000, this process of re-thinking our liturgical expression was greatly strengthened and enriched by the appearance in our midst of Gordon Lathrop and Gail Ramshaw who, as well as being husband and wife, are two of the leading liturgists of the Lutheran tradition in America. Gordon is Professor of Liturgy at the Lutheran Seminary in Philadelphia, and Gail is the Professor of Religion at La Salle University. Gordon was appointed Lutheran Pastor at the cathedral, and the stage was set for the development at the cathedral of a liturgical life that drew on Lutheran as well as Anglican resources, and that would model the Call to Common Mission agreement ratified by both communions in 2000.

Building on our "liturgy of journey," we developed a liturgical approach that translates the baptismal covenant from theory into practice, emphasizing by ritual and gesture the priesthood shared by the people of God. This is not the "priesthood of all believers," which has always suggested to me a "go-it-alone" priesthood of the individual—a notion foreign to the New Testament—but the priesthood of *the community* when it is gathered together for worship, and only then. In this experience of shared priesthood, the ordained presbyterate serves as an enabling sign, calling the community to realize its priestly vocation, but it can never be the totality. Jesus came to free us from sacerdotalism, though we have become awful hard of hearing over the last two thousand years.

To express this shared vocation to priesthood, the presider at the Eucharist vests with the stole, that member called to exercise leadership at any one moment, whether the lector or the preacher or the intercessor. At the table, the whole community is invited to offer the Great Thanksgiving with hands lifted in the *orans* posture of prayer, maintaining a note hummed in harmony with the rest of the community, to undergird the presider's spoken prayer. We experiment with various methods of sharing communion, a favorite being to administer the bread, but to invite members forward to take the cup from the table into their own hands. In these, and in many other gestures and customs we are yet to develop, does the holy priestly community of the people of God come into its own.

3. Designing and Building, 2001

The approach that we developed with our architect George Yu was to take the essential basilican character of Burns' building, and to run with it, emphasizing its good points and reducing the impact of its failings. The original interior was like a picture in a frame, that was also a picture—layer upon layer of decoration and ornamentation that buried the good art and drowned the liturgy that struggled to compete. The forest had been lost in the trees.

The first step was to devise a liturgical layout that would, by using the basilica as a historical reference point, transport the assembly from a Victorian experience of church attendance to a contemporary experience of Christian formation.

The space would be presided over, not by a long-disused relic of a high altar, but by the bishop's chair set in a semi-circular stone *presbyterium* (seating for the presbyters and deacons) found in the earliest

Christian buildings. In a contemporary re-working of that pattern, the *presbyterium* would continue all around the perimeter of the worship space, symbolizing the New Testament insight that all God's people are, through baptism, initiated into the priestly community.

The centrality of baptism as the primary Christian sacrament of consecration (rather than ordination), would be spelt out by a true baptistry (rather than a font with a lid on it), in which water from the old font would cascade continually into a baptismal pool. The baptistry is sited in the south aisle, a funny place for a baptistry you may well say, which should normally be at the entrance. In our case however, the west doors are approached up seven steps from a narrow sidewalk on a busy six-lane highway, and ought not to survive much longer as our primary point of entry into the space. Phase Two of the cathedral project envisages a new gatehouse building on the south side from which all areas and activities of the cathedral site can be accessed. In the meantime, the south aisle will provide a very effective liturgical gathering place around the waters of baptism, from which liturgical journeys of various kinds may set out.

Within the "liturgical arena" of the nave, an ambo would replace lectern and pulpit, and an altar table the stone high altar. The form of the ambo—a long lectern with a bench seat behind it—echoes that of the *bema* of the Jewish synagogue, in a deliberate attempt to speak in a visual language that would help those of other faith traditions to feel at home in our space. In this task, I received invaluable encouragement and advice from my good friend, Rabbi Ivan Caine, for many years rabbi at Philadelphia's Society Hill Synagogue.

The planning of these new liturgical foci required us to face up to the hard questions which are all too often ignored or fudged. "Was it possible to give a new liturgical focus, central to the space, and at the same time retain in place the high altar, albeit as a backdrop to the main space?" For us, the answer was a resounding "No."

No matter how hard we try, a preserved high altar, whatever its qualities as a piece of art, will always shout louder than the new work with which we are attempting to replace it. It will always proclaim a theology of hierarchical division of the assembly and of sacrificial and sacerdotal worship at odds with the teaching of the whole Western church today. Of course, there will be parishes in our neighborhood that, in a period of universal change, will attempt to push the liturgical toothpaste back into the tube. These are places where a lost world is temporarily recaptured, and they have their devotees, but in the final analysis they have no reference point in the catholic world today.

In designing contemporary liturgical spaces, we need to make a choice, and continue the consistent Christian tradition throughout the centuries of clearing out the old to make room for the new. Only during the liturgical revisions of the last thirty years has the church taken to hedging its bets, preferring alternatives to replacements, and it is an approach in which everyone loses.

In our approach therefore, new would replace old without compromise, and furthermore both altar and ambo would be movable to allow different configurations of the space, and chairs would replace pews. Furniture would be kept to a minimum, with chairs stored away when not in use, so that the spaciousness of the renovated space—paved throughout in French limestone—could speak for itself, with the liturgical foci standing out in stark contrast.

Significantly, this essential work of liturgical reconfiguration was something the historical preservationists could understand, even if they could not applaud it, and even if they worried about the fate of particular items of furniture. One further step was required however, a step of equal importance, but one which the preservationists would find difficult to understand.

This step concerned the environment of the liturgical pavement (i.e., the decoration of the "living room" of the people of God assembled to give thanks and praise). To enable the new liturgical scenario to work visually, the interior framework of the building demanded to be made less visually intrusive. In particular, the nave and chancel walls (except for the murals at the east end) required re-coloring if the liturgy, and not the walls, were to draw the eye and take center stage. Originally, the walls were paneled up to around six feet, with muddy brown walls above, stenciled with gold fleur-de-lis. The effect was overpoweringly dismal, and was no fit place for a eucharistic assembly of joyful and abundant life.

The wooden paneling was removed earlier for the construction of the perimeter bench seat and the installation of heating and cooling ducts concealed in a thickened wall up to a height of nine feet. The walls were "Cistercianized" by replacing the busy stencil work with plain walls the color of old plaster, and by removing the intricate "half-timbered" decoration of the clerestory walls. The eleventh-century Cistercian reform of the Benedictine rule, which produced liturgical spaces of matchless beauty devoid of the florid excesses of the earlier period, has much in common with the Anglican emphasis on understatement and restraint. In this respect, the former Church of the Saviour had to be given a helping hand in rediscovering its roots.

New pendant, electric lighting brings illumination to where it is needed, highlighting the liturgical foci and creating an ambience of worship and stillness. Air conditioning (the lack of which has made the old space horribly uncomfortable in humid Philadelphia summers) and a renewed heating system complete the works.

Thus the new interior is an inspiration and a catechetical experience in which we are reminded of our theological inheritance and energized in the expression of our newly rediscovered ministry as members together of the Body of Christ. No longer an audience observing others at work in the "sanctuary" (the term we have used too long in the catholic tradition for the holy of holies beyond the altar rail), we all find ourselves in the sanctuary understood (as our Lutheran and Presbyterian friends have long reminded us) as the whole liturgical space. Here, once we have assembled for worship and for transformation, and not before then, for these are truths revealed to the community of faith *together*, do we reawaken to our call to be that chosen race, that royal priesthood, that holy nation[4] celebrated by the author of the First Letter of Peter.

George Yu likes to say that when he designs a worship space he is building a piano, it is the people of God who must then learn to play this beautiful instrument. In a parallel metaphor, the new cathedral at Philadelphia can be seen as an empty stage on which the assembly of faith will learn to "tread the boards," each member learning, with nervousness but ever-increasing confidence, to play their part without prompting, that the drama of the liturgy may take wings, and the realm of God be re-created as a reality in our midst. In this great drama, it is vital that we do not "lose the plot" amongst the paraphernalia of past ages, but instead inhabit spaces that leave us free and unconfined to explore in worship our relationship to God and to each other.

Fiorello La Guardia, mayor of New York during the 1930s and 1940s, when asked what he was most proud of during his term of office, is known to have said, "That I raised the standard of municipal government everywhere in this country, by raising it in New York and so proving it could be raised." It is our hope likewise that we shall be able to show that transformation of liturgical space is possible everywhere, by showing it is possible here, in this unlikeliest of places, and in this least famous of cathedrals.

In England, many cathedrals have been refurbished and restored with great devotion, skill, and creativity, but only one (of our communion) has been renovated radically in accordance with a theological and liturgical rationale. That cathedral is Portsmouth, where David Stancliffe's inspired work has provided us with a model of how a cathedral can become a space in which the Easter experience comes alive as we move through the space in worship. In the United States, there are many other cathedrals larger, grander and more world-renowned, but if Philadelphia can be for North America what Portsmouth is for England, then it will indeed have made its mark in the most significant way possible.

It goes without saying the entire operation of renovating a worship space, from beginning to end, is in itself merely a first step in the lifetime process of renovating the living stones of our holy priestly community. Carlos Santos-Rivera, pastor of one of the Hispanic congregations in our diocese wrote to me, in the midst of our battles with the preservationists, these moving words: "I wish that the cathedral be always a place where the humble gospel is worshiped and not a theology of structures. I hope that the service to God reflects love for the people and not any fanaticism around a structure. The great scholars think about Victorian structures, but we, the servants of God, think of the victory of the people of God." There really is nothing more to say.

Notes

1. For more by Robert Warren, refer to *Building Missionary Congregations* (London: Church House Publishing, 1995).

2. Sermon 227 (Easter 414) Pal. 38, 1099–1101.

3. The apartment block was eventually purchased by the Church Foundation in December 2001, to secure the possibility of a combined cathedral/diocesan center on the site.

4. 1 Peter 2:9.

Resource Bibliography

The following list contains useful resources that focus on church architecture and liturgical design. It does not pretend to be all inclusive. Only items published or released since 1980 are included to provide a greater likelihood they are available or accessible. In no way is this bibliography intended to dismiss or discredit other resources created prior to that time.

BOOKS

Adams, William Seth. *Moving the Furniture: Liturgical Theory, Practice, and Environment.* New York: Church Publishing Incorporated, 1999.

Archdiocese of Chicago. *Acoustics for Liturgy: A Collection of Articles of The Hymn Society in the U.S. and Canada.* Chicago: Liturgy Training Publications, 1991.

Barrie, Thomas. *Spiritual Path, Sacred Place: Myth, Ritual, and Meaning in Architecture.* Boston: Shambhala, 1996.

Braun, Josef (trans. Linda M. Maloney). *A Little ABC of the Church Interior.* Collegeville, MN: The Liturgical Press, 1997.

Built of Living Stones: Art, Architecture, and Worship: Guidelines of the National Conference of Catholic Bishops. Washington, DC: United States Catholic Conference, Inc., 2000.

Crosbie, Michael J. *Architecture for the Gods.* New York: Watson-Guptill Publications, 2000.

Cunningham, Colin. *Stones of Witness: Church Architecture and Function.* Stroud, UK: Sutton Publishing Limited, 1999.

Cunningham, Pamela. *How Old Is That Church?* London: Blandford, 1990.

DeSanctis, Michael E. *Building From Belief: Advance, Retreat, and Compromise in the Remaking of Catholic Church Architecture.* Collegeville,

MN: The Liturgical Press, 2002.

DeSanctis, Michael E. *Renewing the City of God: Catholic Architectural Reform in the United States.* Chicago: Liturgical Training Publications, 1994.

Dilasser, Maurice (trans. Mary Cabrini Durkin, Madeleine Beaumont, and Caroline Morson). *The Symbols of the Church.* Collegeville, MN: The Liturgical Press, 1999.

Foley, Edward. *From Age to Age: How Christians Celebrated the Eucharist.* Chicago: Liturgy Training Publications, 1991.

Fulton, Charles N., Patrick J. Holtkamp and Fritz Frurip. *The Church for Common Prayer: A Statement on Worship Space for the Episcopal Church.* New York: The Episcopal Church Building Fund, 1994.

Fulton, Charles N. and Patrick J. Holtkamp. *Church Sites and Buildings.* New York: The Episcopal Church Building Fund, 1991.

Galley, Howard E. "Of Churches and Their Furnishings" *The Ceremonies of the Eucharist: A Guide to Celebration.* Cambridge, MA: Cowley Publications (1989) 2–17.

Giles, Richard. *Re-Pitching the Tent: Re-ordering the Church Building for Worship and Mission.* Revised and expanded edition Norwich, UK: The Canterbury Press, 1999.

Holeton, David R., ed. *Our Thanks and Praise: The Eucharist in Anglicanism Today: Papers from the Fifth International Anglican Liturgical Consultation.* Toronto: Anglican Book Centre, 1998.

Huffman, Walter C. and S. Anita Stauffer. *Where We Worship.* Minneapolis: Augsburg Publishing House, 1987.

Kieckhefer, Richard. *Metaphors Built of Stone: Church Architecture and Its Liturgical Meanings.* New York: Oxford University Press, forthcoming.

Koenig, John. *The Feast of the World's Redemption: Eucharistic Origins and Christian Mission.* Valley Forge, PA: Trinity Press International, 2000.

Mauck, Marchita. *Places for Worship: A Guide to Building and Renovating.* (American Essays Liturgy; Edward Foley, series ed.)

Collegeville, MN: The Liturgical Press, 1995.

Mauck, Marchita. *Shaping a House for the Church.* Chicago: Liturgy Training Publications, 1990.

McNorgan, David. *Preparing the Environment for Worship.* Collegeville, MN: The Liturgical Press, 1997.

Middleton, Arthur Pierce. *New Wine in Old Skins: Liturgical Change and the Setting of Worship.* Wilton, CT: Morehouse-Barlow, 1988.

Norman, Edward R. *The House of God: Church Architecture, Style, and History.* New York: Thames and Hudson, 1990.

Ogasapian, John K. *Church Organs: A Guide to Selection and Purchase.* Grand Rapids, MI: Baker Book House, 1983.

Pfatteicher, Philip H. "Architecture: Hallowing Space." *Liturgical Spirituality.* Valley Forge, PA: Trinity Press International (1997) 142–173.

The Place of Worship: Pastoral Directory on the Building and Reordering of Churches. Third Edition Dublin, Ireland: Veritas Publications; Carlow, Ireland: Irish Institute of Pastoral Liturgy, 1994.

Purdy, Martin Terence. *Churches and Chapels: A Design and Development Guide.* London; Boston: Butterworth Architecture, 1991.

Ray, David R. "The Worship Space Shapes the Worship and the People." *Wonderful Worship in Smaller Churches.* Cleveland: The Pilgrim Press, (2000) 129–135.

Rouet, Albert, (trans. Paul Philibert). "Ecclesial Space." *Liturgy and the Arts.* Collegeville, MN: The Liturgical Press (1997) 89–121.

Schloeder, Steven J. *Architecture in Communion: Implementing the Second Vatican Council through Liturgy and Architecture.* San Francisco: Ignatius Press, 1998.

Simons, Thomas G. and James M. Fitzpatrick. *The Ministry of Liturgical Environment.* Collegeville, MN: The Liturgical Press, 1984.

Visser, Margaret. *The Geometry of Love: Space, Time, Mystery, and Meaning in an Ordinary Church.* New York: North Point Press; Farrar, Straus and Giroux, 2000.

Vosko, Richard. *Through the Eye of a Rose Window: A Perspective on the Enviroment for Worship.* Saratoga, CA: Resource Publications, 1981.

White, James F. "Liturgical Architecture." *Christian Worship in North America: A Retrospective: 1955–1995.* Collegeville, MN: The Liturgical Press; A Pueblo Book (1997) 211–291.

White, James F. "The Language of Space." *Introduction to Christian Worship.* Nashville: Abingdon Press (1983, 5th printing) 76–109.

White, James F. and Susan J. White. *Church Architecture: Building and Renovating for Christian Worship.* Nashville, TN: Abingdon Press, 1988.

Wilson-Kastner, Patricia. "People, Time, and Space: The Inclusive Community: Liturgical Space." *Sacred Drama: A Spirituality of Christian Liturgy.* Minneapolis: Fortress Press (1999) 42–47.

ESSAYS IN COLLECTIONS

Hatchett, Marion. "The Architectural Implications of the Book of Common Prayer." *The Occasional Papers of the Standing Liturgical Commission, Collection Number One.* New York: Church Hymnal Corporation (1987) 57–66.

Stancliffe, David. "A Cathedral for Pilgrims." *Forever Building,* ed. Sarah Quail and Alan Wilkinson. Portsmouth, UK: Portsmouth Cathedral Council (1995) 143–157.

Stancliffe, David. "Creating Sacred Space: Liturgy and Architecture Interacting." *The Sense of the Sacramental: Movement and Measure in Art and Music, Place and Time,* ed. David Brown and Ann Loades. London: SPCK (1995) 44–58.

White, Susan. "The Theology of Sacred Space." *The Sense of the Sacramental: Movement and Measure in Art and Music, Place and Time,* ed. David Brown and Ann Loades. London: SPCK (1995) 31–43.

Articles in Periodicals

Brown, Bill. "The Process of Building." *Liturgy* 5:4 (1986): 15–23.

Brown, Bill. "Despite Its Strong Points, I Wonder about This Chapter." *Pastoral Music* 25:5 (June–July 2001): 44–47.

Clutz, Charles N. "Acoustics Reassessed: An Opportunity." *The American Organist* (December 1987): 70–71.

Ferguson, Philip L. "So You Are Going To Build...." *Reformed Liturgy and Music* 31:3 (1997): 190–194.

Fleisher, Dennis. "Concerns for Pastoral Musicians in Built of Living Stones." *Pastoral Music* 25:5 (June–July 2001): 29–35.

Frenning, Carol. "Predesign: A Teachable Moment." *The Clergy Journal* 74:1 (October 1997): 11–14.

Griffin, Benjammin. "Theology and Architecture." *The Clergy Journal* 74:1 (October 1997): 8–10.

Horrigan, J. Philip. "Conversation Partners Form a Holy People." *Pastoral Music* 25:5 (June–July 2001): 24–28.

Huffman, Robert. "The Concept of Sacred Space." *Liturgy* 5:4 (1986): 43–45.

Huffman, Walter C. "Living Stones: Space to Proclaim the Gospel." *Reformed Liturgy and Music* 31:3 (1997): 183–189.

Jung, Henry. "Are Perfect Church Acoustics Possible?" *Faith & Form* 14 (Spring 1980): 15–18.

Madden, Lawrence J., S.J. "Designing Space for Celebrating Eucharist." *Initiative Report: Catholic Common Ground Initiative* 5:2 (June 2001): 3–11.

Malarcher, Willy. "The Climate of Worship" *Liturgy* 5:4 (1986): 67–69.

Mantle, John. "Early Bird with Early English: Theology, Culture, and Church Design." *Theology* 94:761 (1991): 349–354.

Mauck, Marchita C. "Buildings That House the Church." *Liturgy* 5:4 (1986): 25–33.

Mauck, Marchita C. "The Shape of the Rites." *Liturgy* 5:4 (1986): 71–75.

McManus, Frederick R. "The Setting for Christian Worship." *Liturgy* 5:4 (1986): 7–13.

Notebaart, James. "The Font and the Assembly." *Liturgy* 5:4 (1986): 59–65.

Partington, David C. and Sally W. Gant. "Our Place to Be." *Reformed Liturgy and Music* 31:3 (1997): 167–172.

Raguin, Virginia Chieffo. "Change, Movement, and Expectation in Church Art." *Pastoral Music* 25:5 (June–July 2001): 38–43.

Rambusch, Robert. "Creating a House for the Church." *Liturgy* 5:4 (1986): 47–49.

Reeder, Rachel. "Perfect in Beauty." *Liturgy* 5,4 (1986): 5.

Riedel, Scott R. "Good Acoustics." *The Living Church* 185:20 (November 14, 1982): 10–11.

Seasoltz, R. Kevin. "Transcendence and Immanence in Sacred Art and Architecture." *Worship* 75:5 (September 2001): 403–431.

Sikula, Arthur J. "Questions about Guiding Themes." *Pastoral Music* 25:5 (June–July 2001): 17–23.

Sovik, Edward A. "Church Architecture—A Public Language." *Liturgy* 4:4 (1985): 83–89.

Stauffer, S. Anita. "A Place for Burial, Birth and Bath." *Liturgy* 5:4 (1986): 51–57.

Teig, Mons A. "Worship in Space." *The Clergy Journal* 74:1 (October 1997): 4–7.

Torgerson, Mark A. "Gathering at the Table of Promise and Joy: Reflections on Eucharistic Space." *Reformed Liturgy and Music* 31:3 (1997): 163–166.

Wetherill, Ewart A. "Acoustics for Worship." *The American Organist* 30:8 (August 1996): 60–64.

PERIODICALS

Church Building, Gabriel Communications Ltd., Manchester, UK;
(phone) 0161 236 8856, (fax) 0161 236 8530).

*E&A, Environment & Art Letter: A Forum on Architecture and the Arts for
the Parish,* Liturgy Training Publications, Chicago, IL;
www.ltp.org; 1-800-933-1800.

Faith and Form, Journal of the Interfaith Forum on Religion, Art and
Architecture, Washington, DC.

Sacred Architecture, Notre Dame, IN; 703-437-8432.

VIDEOTAPES

Churches for Common Prayer: Building for the Liturgical Assembly. New
York: Episcopal Church Building Fund, no date.

Stauffer, S. Anita, *Re-examining baptismal fonts: Baptismal space for the
contemporary church* Collegeville, MN: Liturgical Press, 1991.

INTERNET WEBSITES

Church Architecture (www.churcharchitecture.net)

Church of England Church Care (www.churchcare.co.uk)

The Ecclesiological Society (www.ecclsoc.org)

Episcopal Church Building Fund (www.ECBF.org)

The Episcopal Church and Visual Arts (www.ecva.org)

Georgetown Center for Liturgy (www.georgetown.edu/centers/gcl)

Partners for Sacred Places (www.sacredplaces.org)

Contributors

William Seth Adams is the J. Milton Richardson Professor of Liturgics and Anglican Studies at the Episcopal Theological Seminary of the Southwest in Austin, Texas, since 1982. He holds degrees from Bexley Hall and Princeton University. As a member of the Environment and Art Study Group of the North American Academy of Liturgy, he convenes the Anglican members of the Academy. He is the author of *Moving the Furniture: Liturgical Theory, Practice, and Environment* (1999) and *Shaped by Images: One Who Presides* (1995).

Michael Battle is the Assistant Professor of Spirituality and Black Church Studies at Duke University Divinity School, and Rector of St. Ambrose Episcopal Church in Raleigh, North Carolina. Currently, he also serves as chaplain to the House of Bishops of the Episcopal Church.

Carol Doran is Professor of Music and Liturgy, as well as the seminary organist at the Virginia Theological Seminary in Alexandria, Virginia. Formerly on the faculty of Bexley Hall in Rochester, New York, she developed the Master of Divinity with concentration in Pastoral Music degree program. She is a composer of music for hymnody, the co-author of two hymnals, and writer of numerous other books and articles on music.

Brantley W. Gasaway received his B.A. in Religion from the College of William and Mary and M.A. in Comparative Religion from Miami University. Awarded the Renick Scholarship in International Studies from William and Mary, he traveled for two months in England to study historic Anglican parish church architecture. He is currently enrolled in the doctoral program in Religious Studies at the University of North Carolina-Chapel Hill, focusing on the historic and contemporary relationship between Protestant Evangelicals and Roman Catholics.

214

Richard Giles is Dean of Philadelphia Cathedral in the Episcopal Diocese of Pennsylvania. He is the author of *Re-pitching the Tent, We do not Presume,* and *Mark my Word.* Prior to coming to this country, he served as the Parish Development Officer and Canon Theologian for the Diocese of Wakefield, England.

J. Derek Harbin serves as a member of the church planting team for Church of the Beloved, a new Episcopal congregation in Charlotte, North Carolina. A priest for fourteen years, he received his M.Div. from Nashotah House and D.Min. in Congregational Development from Seabury-Western, where he serves on the adjunct faculty of Seabury Institute.

W. Brown Morton III is Priest Associate at Grace Episcopal Church, in The Plains, Virginia. He holds the Prince B. Woodard Chair in Historic Preservation at Mary Washington College in Fredericksburg, Virginia. He is an international architectural conservator, whose most recent project involves developing recommendations for the protection of the Memorial of Moses at Mt. Nebo in Jordan. He also is the co-author of *The Secretary of the Interior's Standards for Historic Preservation Projects.*

David Philippart, Editor of *E&A Environment and Art Letter,* has a degree in liturgical studies from the University of Notre Dame and lives in Chicago, Illinois.

John Ander Runkle is the Associate Rector of Christ Episcopal Church in Roanoke, Virginia. Prior to being ordained, he practiced architecture for over twelve years, specializing in historic structures. He received his M.Div. from the University of the South and B.Arch. from the University of Tennessee/Knoxville.

Donald Schell has worked, since 1980, in team with Rick Fabian as vicars and now rectors of St. Gregory of Nyssa Episcopal Church in San Francisco, California. As the current church building was being designed and built, he served as co-chair of the building committee and as the "owner's representative." He is a member of the Council of Associated Parishes for Liturgy and Mission. Along with his daughter, Maria, he wrote *My Father, My Daughter: Pilgrims on the Road to Santiago.*

David H. Smart, a priest in the Diocese of Ontario, Canada, holds a doctoral degree in liturgy with specialization in the question of liturgical space.

David Stancliffe is Bishop of Salisbury, England, and former Provost of Portsmouth, where he completed and re-ordered the cathedral. He served as Vice President of the European Cathedrals Association, member of the Council for the Care of Churches, and then of the Cathedrals' Fabric Commission. He is a member of the Church of England Liturgical Commission and has been its chairman since 1992.

Susan J. White is the Harold L. and Alberta H. Lunger Professor of Spiritual Resources and Disciplines at Brite Divinity School, Texas Christian University. She previously served as lecturer and tutor in Liturgics at Westcott House, Cambridge (UK), and as a member of the Church of England Liturgical Commission.